I0667892

SERPENT CLUB PRESS
NEW WRITING
SUMMER '24

Edited by Matthew Gasda, Paul Franz & Rob Gittings

SERPENT CLUB PRESS
NEW WRITING
SUMMER '24

Printed in the United States of America
Designed & formatted by Anastasia Wolfe
Cover image by August Lamm

TABLE OF CONTENTS

Memoir Excerpt: Fragments of Virginia Life

Mike Crumplar

Back in the days I spent reading incel texts, the pandemic, the endless boredom in isolation, the arboreal provincial capital of DC, before NYC, before clout life before white supremacist egirls before nihilism fascists there was that provincial capital between yankee and dixie, the covert capital, repressed suburban metropolis of secrets and double lives and spy dead drops and during the day we smoked weed in parks that were gay cruising honeypot ops by night, but it was all still so sexless, I had a trajectory like a normal but underachieving Virginia bourgeois, sheltered suburban childhood to university graduate to 9-5 job in DC, the NGO-complex, the nonprofit complex clerk, office drone in sexless bro world, that's why I was drawn to the incels, the sexless loser men who lash out and go on killing sprees to punish the world for denying them access to that supposedly limitless carnal pleasure promised to bourg white men in all their privilege. I was also drawn to trouble, would always roll with the troublemakers, there was B, and for some reason I wanted to be a writer, maybe just wanted attention, maybe it was just the only art I could actually do, whatever it was it came from a place of resentment. The theory of the incels: white man resentment studies. This is just like *Notes from Underground*, I said of the Elliot Rodger manifesto, Elliot Rodger's Hollywood life even appeared glamorous from Virginia. Everyone can make themselves an expert, a scholar on Twitter. Everyone can play that part. They can download endless PDFs of philosophy and literary theory and miscellaneous esoterica and juxtapose screenshots of those paragraphs with detritus of internet culture. And the internet detritus salon culture was particularly thriving in that era, the Trump era that brought the Dimes Square freaks to CPAC. I had so little of real life outside the sheltered Virginia bubble that I had to seek out novelty online, weird characters, troublemakers, who were inspiring. This is what writers are supposed to do. Meet the people, but also feud with them. They're always wrong, and though they might have some common interest with me, those shared hyperfixations, they go about it in the wrong way. It bothered me. Something about their enjoyment in their wrongness was annoying. This feeling motivated countless polemics. There were years of this incel creative life, most of it a projection, a bit to win an audience, to become someone whose opinion some people somewhere cared about, but between the bursts of productivity were interminable spells of boredom, isolation, stasis, total misanthropy, total disgust with the people around me, and yet, I was from their class, a product of this whole hideous provincialism, but I always fantasized about shooting them, like the incels, but my sexlessness was more "sophisticated," more sophisticated than simply the frustration of getting no pussy, it was about recognition, culture, "the beautiful" and from there the beautiful revealed itself in, for example, the political moment, the George Floyd uprising, something that seemed to break apart the continuum of everyday mundane fascist drone existence, the smashed windows in Georgetown, the graffiti, the new solidarity in the streets, the unthinkable, riotous utopia...

***

2016. In Virginia I fantasize about becoming a respected writer. I commute to DC to copyedit World Bank reports about streamlining trade in Africa and preparing for climate catastrophe, the end of the world. Bored and on Adderall, I make use of my German Studies degree by posing as a public intellectual on Twitter. I become an expert on Spinoza. I write aphorisms about how some forgettable Soundcloud rapper is like Novalis. I post screenshots of poems from obscure PDFs. I expand my audience by arguing with other self-styled autodidact philosophers who have dilettantish readings of writers I had read in college. Some people get the idea that I'm a grad student or a professor, but they are wrong. The autodidacts annoy me because I see something of myself in them—petty bourgeois white men, misanthropic underachievers, bitter mediocrities with no future. That familiarity is how I play a troll and an infiltrator into the Twitter Cosmic Circle. Some of these former gifted kids imagine themselves becoming court philosophers for a future fascist regime. They see themselves as Heidegger, posting memes from their humble Swabian cottage, Trump their Hitler. Trump will complete the system of German Idealism, one inane mantra among many that they tell their tens of thousands of troll followers, who really just want some veneer of intellectualism to validate their bigotries. Many of my self-serious rivals in the Cosmic Circle periodically have public meltdowns whenever they realize how badly their "visions" have been misunderstood—either by their followers or their comrades—and the inevitable fallings-out are vicious and amusing. Most of them are far too volatile ever to get close to real power and influence. On Twitter they write a sort of fan fiction about real life— though it's not so much about real life as it is about the spectacle of politics, which is not so much about politics as it is about spectacle. A way to make watching the news more fun. When Trump wins, some of the autodidacts reveal themselves in the flesh, geeks marching through the streets of New York among the weeping protestors, boasting in a viral video that their Twitter activity set the Machtergreifung in motion with computer magic. They posted their way to transcendental agency in the samsaric nightmare of history, mystical pundit-mouthpieces of the new regime. The end times are here. Or so they hope. Ephemeral nerds. The only thing that will be of lasting interest about them is how they mythologize this inverted world. I bully them, but they are bullies too. I make myself a target for their ridicule, I play along. So goes the hustle, the humiliation, the discourse. On the internet, this is how I build a brand, and building a brand is a necessary step in becoming a writer.

***

During this time I live in Arlington with Eduardo, a friend from college. A comrade. Eduardo is an ad-man who believes in the bullshit of brands, like a drug dealer hopelessly addicted to his own stash. He buys lots of things from J.Crew because he believes that he lives up to the lifestyle of that brand, he told me. "I get it all on sale because I follow this blog about bros dressing well basically. It's a blog that says how to dress well and get the best brands on sale so anyone can dress well." Eduardo loves ideologies. Some of his favorites: Libertarianism, Masculinity, the Old South, Catholicism, the band Tool. He is also interested in gender studies—he's redpilled, and he watches the Evangelist of Masculinity on Youtube, among countless other gurus. Eduardo admires how the Evangelist eviscerates the female gender. He's like the Robert E. Lee of crushing pussy, a once-in-a-generation tactical genius. The Evangelist knows what women really want. Women are quite simple, and their machinations are all part of an intricate game. The relationship between men and women is very physical, very primordial, it can be diagrammed as a geometry of power and influence, a chess game.

Eduardo shows me a Youtube video. The Evangelist of Masculinity is talking to a girl. She is standing in front of a crowd, crying. Does she love her ex? Or her current boyfriend? She's unsatisfied, and she needs someone who knows what she wants. The Evangelist of Masculinity is a hunk, and he knows how to rat out just what it is that she needs. "Is he too... feminine?" he asks about her boyfriend. Sobbing, she nods. He hit it on the head, as always. Eduardo nods in unison. "This here is the good shit, he just knows how to read people," he says, "It's the geometry, the power geometry." Get on the phone now, says the Evangelist in his deep voice, his deep soothing voice. The woman takes out her cell phone, and the crowd watches her. "You can do it," the Evangelist assures her. His microphone amplifies his booming voice; under her mic, her frailty is all the more apparent. In a trance, she presses speed dial. Speaker phone. After a few moments, a man on the other end picks up. "Mark, baby, I love you, it's not you it's me. I need someone who gives me what I want. We can't be. We just can't be." The man on the other end hangs up. The crowd bursts into applause. The woman's tears, an orgasmic crescendo. The Evangelist is nodding with that manly frown of righteousness. This had to be done, it had to be done to give her what she wanted. She doesn't want an effeminate man. He would just leech off her. The effeminate man is a parasite. She needed someone to unleash her, unleash her desire like a wildfire onto the world, burning the wretched undergrowth of dead forests. A righteous wildfire, burning the whole world in sacred flame. "This is the good shit," says Eduardo, "He just can read people so well. He's a damn magician."

One time Eduardo got in an argument with a girl on Facebook in the comments beneath a Trump meme he posted. "I so owned her when she blocked me," he said. "You need to make a Facebook group for this and set it to private," I told him. "That's a great idea," he replied, "I'm such a damn shitlord, I simply cannot be stopped. I will make the group immediately." He made the group and added me, and I used it as a place to post the treasures I'd find probing the depths of the internet. "Get this damn meme off my page," he says to me, "this is NSFW." The meme is a picture of a guy doing a BMX stunt at night and in the background the camera flash catches both a group of dogs fucking and a guy sucking another dude off. I used a meme-generator website to add a non sequitur message about Trump. "It's a great image," I tell him, "It's great content. This is what the internet is for. The internet needs to transgress boundaries, it needs to question authoritarian structures. This is great content. Revolutionary content, even. The true spirit of 2016."

Eduardo liked fucking Loretta because she's from the South. She might be dumb as bricks, and a Hillary voter, but there's something persistently virginal about her. He's a Catholic, of course, but he's got a soft spot for the Baptist types, he likes their little quirks and prejudices. Loretta's mom didn't like Eduardo at first, not because he's Latino but because he's Catholic, and he found that charming.

Catholicism is very concerned with images, icons. It's just as concerned with the Truth as it is with the sensuous thing, Eduardo told me. I was raised Catholic, too, but I'm a gringo. I can have a vague sense of the Truth of Catholicism only because I dated a passionate Latina once myself.

Catholicism goes well with promiscuity. The Truth of stereotypes: Catholic schoolgirls, Catholic priests, and so on. Mary is very womanly, very virginal. Loretta is so virginal. The saints are movie stars. You can fuck all you want and go to penance and it's cleared. Think of all those macho Latino guys out at the clubs, wild and shit, fucking and leaving spicy Latina bitches, dropping them before they get too involved. And that's good, because more often than not they're simply that, crazy bitches. And then the spicy Latina bitches go to church with their mothers, crying in the bosoms of their mothers—just like Latin men and their mothers, Latin men and the wives they find who then become their crazy Latin mothers, taking the place of their actual Latin mothers—and it's all forgiven. The crazy sluts become virginal again. That's Catholicism, for sure. You just can't do abortions—but sex, that's encouraged. Think of all the seductive dancing, going to the clubs and then getting pushy with girls, who are generally very horny. That is a Catholic culture. But it is cognitive-dissonant, because it comes with guilt, because sex is bad, it's sinful. But Eduardo likes that, the paradoxical obsession with fallenness, because it is dramatic. He will cry so much when his mother dies, he says.

Eduardo and Loretta shared a mutual understanding that sex was sinful. But he wanted sex from Loretta, and she didn't want to give it. They didn't fuck at first. Loretta said she was sexually assaulted when she was younger, but he's not sure if she was telling the truth or whatnot. You know, girls lie or exaggerate about this sort of thing. You can't believe girls about these things unless they have real evidence. Maybe he didn't want to believe her because he was unsettled by the idea that she had more sexual experience than him. He was a virgin before fucking her. Eventually, once they did start fucking, she was all about it, and they did it a lot. She even wanted to fuck in a deserted barn on the highway while driving back from her parents' place. This disgusted Eduardo, it was unclean, it was kinky, perhaps even a bit fruity. After a while, Loretta basically dried up again. She didn't want sex anymore. That's when she had the power, the power to withhold sex. She had it because sex was what kept them together and once she had Eduardo, she didn't need sex anymore. He had to find a way to get the power back, to have the leverage over her. He had to find what she wanted. He couldn't want, he couldn't have any absence. To be wanting and not to have, to be desperate—that is effeminate. It turns the woman off. The woman wants the sense of security of the man, she wants him to be a good provider. But he could never figure out how to get her to put out again, and they broke up.

After Eduardo broke up with Loretta, he went on the apps. When he had a hard time getting matches, he joined a "leadership community for entrepreneurs, creatives, and innovative professionals who are passionate about making a lasting positive impact." He had to pay a couple thousand dollars in annual dues, but that gave him access to exclusive events. He said it was like a fraternity for adults, with lots of great networking for business leaders. He started bringing home cougars. Senior executives, consultants, politicos. They were more intellectual than younger women like Loretta. He needed to get his money's worth of pussy, since he already had a $20,000 credit card debt. He started drinking pomegranate juice so that he could produce more sperm.

One night he told me he was going to meet with Loretta, he was going to try to fuck her again. He saw her post on Facebook that she was going to China for a year—she speaks Mandarin and got into some sort of exchange program for her job—and he messaged her "good luck!" and "have fun!" She asked if he wanted to get brunch and he said yes, but only because he wants to fuck her, he told me, so he told her he's not doing brunch but can meet after. She said no, it can only be brunch. He told her he couldn't do brunch. "I'm not gonna do brunch because then I can't fuck her," he told me. But she wouldn't meet otherwise. So he was like, alright yeah let's do brunch. I said Eduardo she's not gonna fuck you, that's the reason you guys broke up. "Well, she's gonna think differently when she sees me." We had a long conversation. "Well, yeah, maybe I'm lying to myself just because I want to see her. Actually, I don't want to see her, but it's the right thing to do. Seeing her. I mean, we dated for three years, after all." Then he had brunch with her, and they didn't fuck.

***

On the internet, I become an amateur psychoanalytic literary theorist. I become an expert in incel studies. I am convinced that the incels symbolize something significant about the alienation of modern life and contemporary sexuality and bourgeois ideology and whatever. The internet turns us all into loathsome incels, in some sense. My "doctoral thesis," an unfinished critical exegesis of My Twisted World, the manifesto of the 2014 Isla Vista mass shooter, Elliot Rodger. My "thesis advisor," a local philosophy professor I meet on Twitter. The professor leads a Deleuze **Anti-Oedipus** reading group that meets at Comet Ping-Pong, a primary site in the Pizzagate conspiracy imaginary. He initiates me into the mysteries of Lacanian thought. At first he suspects that I'm a cryptofascist because of my interest in Nick Land and accelerationism, which are in vogue on Twitter at the time, particularly in the Cosmic Circle. I start an email correspondence with Slavoj Žižek. I get his attention by saying that I'm a leftist who is too interested in weird politically incorrect ideas for the proper leftist spaces and then he copies excerpts of my emails into his op-eds, referring to me as his "incel friend."

My Twisted World is not a manifesto, I argue, it is a bildungsroman. It is a novel that tells the story of one's formative years or spiritual education, a coming-of-age story. The story of how Elliot Rodger came to be an incel. It's a heroic foundation myth.

I am invited to give a lecture on my research at a Georgetown University fraternity house. "We're dying as an organization, but that's also why I have the freedom to set this up," the guy tells me. The event is called "The Discourse on the Incels," and I advertise it on Twitter. The frat house is an elegant, if now somewhat decrepit, building from the Reconstruction era.

In attendance are the professor and about three dozen other Twitter followers and Georgetown undergraduates—all men, most of them clearly eccentric. My first experience of being a niche internet microcelebrity. I bring my full annotated printout of *My Twisted World*. The lecture begins. Some of the listeners take notes. Some listeners take pictures on their cell phones. In the question-and-answer period, I am asked about the possibility of a cure for the incels. After the lecture, about a dozen of us go to a nearby bar. Then I go back home to Arlington.

***

I'm sitting on the couch at the apartment smoking weed and reading posts on incel forums when Eduardo comes strutting in after a weekend in Charlottesville. He's got with him a bunch of bottles of Trump wine. Eduardo tells me about the beauty of Charlottesville, the rolling hills of the Virginia piedmont that he just experienced on his drunk drive back, an aristocratic landscape, a landscape that spawns great generals and statesmen, rolling pastures, equestrian country, sundress horse girls, yes, they dress up in Charlottesville (that's one thing he likes about them, those UVA bastards, even though they're our rivals but they love to dress up), he saw some article recently about how all these New York influencers are going down to "live an Italian summer in Virginia," frolicking around neoclassical columns of Monticello, the yankee girl yearns for a true American renaissance, in the cradle of a civilization built on tobacco, memories of a golden age, an age of enlightenment, no better place for that than the American Salò I tell him, anyway, he was on the Corner with his bros last night drunk off bourbon and he let slip the raw masculine id when he started talking about Trump to some sundress sluts, I'm such a damn shitlord, he says, usually he'd rather have a good time with the bros and not abandon them, by the time he spends enough time with his friends he's usually just too drunk to hit on girls and just ends up bringing up Trump because he's such a damn shitlord, they get mad triggered, that's why the raw masculine id needs to be contained under the mask of gentility, the eternal necessity of masks, yes, imagine the raw passion of Robert E. Lee when he steps down from the horse, when the elegant white gloves came off, maybe the real sin of Lost Cause hagiography was just that it concealed what a pussyhound he had to have been, an erotic god, like Don Draper, like The Donald, the ultimate Donald, an intense node of masculine polarity, of course there was a reason for that obfuscation, the cucked city-slicking yankee carpetbagger spirit couldn't tolerate it, this noble masculine dharma had to take an esoteric form, a lost truth for a lost cause, the surrender at Appomattox nothing less than a crime against Truth and Beauty, no, this is not a place of honor, Grant that greasy goblin, slouched and shaking, how he must've stunk of booze sweat and death and modernity, and in the hundred-fifty-something years since we've seen the long rise of the federal state and the tyranny of the weak over the noble, the accumulation of perpetual debt, financialization, the virile yeoman shackled by the birth of a yankee debtor nation, the mathematical dialectic, that's the real apocalypse of the industrial world, not global warming but the cuckolding of the colonial planter aristocracy of North America, the closest thing the Anglo had to the hacienda lifestyle (Washington, Jefferson, Lee—even Trump with his wineries and golf courses, spiritual successors of the plantation—all honorary Latinos), out out out, he says, mimicking The Donald, out with Hamilton the prime snot in all American history (Pound, *Cantos*, LXII) and out with the Federal Reserve and out with the treachery of mercantile Britain and out with the yankee rape of the South and out with Crooked Hillary and out with the ghost Tinderellas of the DMV area, all this was what he contemplated on his way back from Charlottesville as the Trump wine settled in his stomach and the sun set over Shenandoah and he approached the Fairfax sprawl, the pussyless return to yankee urban life, the federal life, the debtor's life, he thought about the rustic elegance of the Trump winery, and how ironic it is that the great man himself doesn't drink.

I always felt some pity, perhaps even contempt, from Eduardo when he'd come back to see me high on the couch with the grinder and bong and weed out. It was unclean. Maybe I reminded him of Grant—slouched, stinking, eyes sunken and bloodshot, eminently dishonorable. Yes, Eduardo was the alcoholic, but he was a functioning, extroverted one. There's a place for that in respectable DC society. He wasn't really part of respectable DC society, but at least he had the hope that he could somehow climb into it, he was just one happy hour away from the right connection. I was the stoner recluse, a total dead end. At best, a curiosity. But whatever charm a young stoner might have will inevitably run out, especially in such a place as DC, where the norm is to start acting like a forty-year-old dad right out of college. Weed was feminizing, passive, it signified my refusal to become a man. Still, Eduardo would always ask me to smoke him out. He didn't buy weed himself, he was afraid of doing that. He worried that he'd get caught, like George Michael in that park bathroom. It could be career-ruining. He didn't trust the DC delivery services and didn't want to give out his phone number. I had the weed stash, he had the booze stash. The staples: Miller Lite, Trump wine, and an admittedly impressive array of high-end whiskey, bourbon, scotch, rye, cognac…

***

A heron flies over a small artificial lake on a golf course in a gated McMansion community in the peripheral exurbs of Prince William County, Virginia.

"You can tell a lot about someone by looking at their books," my dad says as he turns to the bookshelf in his office. He scans the titles, as if he's only just realized the implication of what he just said and is now curious what it says about him. At a glance: complete six-volume hardcover sets of Winston Churchill's *The World Crisis* and *The Second World War*; an extensive collection of other books about World War I (with a particular focus on the Eastern Front and pre-war diplomatic machinations); an extensive collection of other books about World War II (again with a particular focus on the Eastern Front, naval campaigns in the Pacific, some rather technical books about aviation and naval armaments); an extensive collection of books about the American Civil War (Shelby Foote's three-volume set, James McPherson's *Battle Cry of Freedom*, Eric Foner's *Reconstruction*, Ron Chernow's biography of Grant, numerous others about individual battles and campaigns, a collection of Marx's journalism on the subject, a presumably-ironic antique copy of Edward A. Pollard's *The Lost Cause*, and so on); books about the Franco-Prussian War (including a biography of Bismarck, Émile Zola's novel *The Debacle*, and Alistair Horne's *The Fall of Paris*—not to mention Horne's other books on other subjects); books about British colonial wars (Opium Wars, Crimean War, Sepoy Mutiny, Zulu Wars, Boer Wars, Boxer Rebellion, and so on); books about the Napoleonic Wars (unmistakably Anglophilic: War of the Sixth Coalition, Battle of Waterloo, biography of the Duke of Wellington); a few books about Frederick the Great; Dumas Malone's six-volume biography of Thomas Jefferson; Chateaubriand's *Memoirs from Beyond the Grave*; Henry Kissinger's *Diplomacy*, *On China*, and *A World Restored: Metternich, Castlereagh and the Problems of Peace 1812–1822*; Trotsky's *History of the Russian Revolution,* translated by Max Eastman (probably the only book from Haymarket Press); Joseph Conrad's *Heart of Darkness*, *Lord Jim*, and *Under Western Eyes*; Ernst Jünger's *Storm of Steel,* Remarque's *All Quiet on the Western Front*, several of the *Flashman* novels; recent geopolitics books about contemporary Russia and China, books by Putin-whisperers who write for *The Atlantic*; and so on. He strokes his chin. "Huh... a lot of books about war."

There are also a bunch of disposable bestsellers about Donald Trump. As always, the conversation with my dad comes back to Trump. Trump is the end of the world, the undoing of my dad's life's work. Every day the paper gives him news of a new national disgrace. He is a single-issue voter, and that issue is imperialism. Pax Americana: NATO, Atlanticism, the special relationship with Britain, the presence of American troops in Europe and Japan and Korea, the Five Eyes alliance (and Zionism, though Trump's embrace of the most chauvinistic Zionist hardliners suddenly complicates that, the insanity of the colonial endeavor can no longer be concealed). Trump makes the nation unreliable, a laughingstock, undermining America's relations with its allies and discrediting American leadership. The imperial body has no head. The decline of American leadership is the decline of civilization, which must be defended by great, erudite men—men who grasp the magnitude of world history. If only America had a leader like Churchill. Russia is already on Europe's doorstep, my dad says, Europe's doorstep! They'll take the Baltics, and Trump won't care. He'll unilaterally destroy NATO. Decades of credibility lost. That's what Trump wants! Trump doesn't care about history. Maybe he'll use the atomic bomb. Not for good reason, but like a Caesar, like MacArthur. (His father, my grandfather, administered the occupation of Japan under MacArthur, and then for some time afterwards, and that's where dad was born, "American soil" on the island of Honshu…) MacArthur was a genuine threat to democracy. And he was a real war hero. It was good to fire him—a decisive moment. At stake: the primacy of the Constitution, the authority of the president, civilian control of the military. Now the roles are reversed, and dad can only hope that the joint chiefs can rein in the civilian Caesar. The Caesar of appeasers. Trump wouldn't care if the Russians marched all the way to Paris. He'd simply shrug and ask what's in it for him. Illiterate moron. Bush was never this bad. No appreciation for duty. He'd say Europe deserves it for not paying him more. The Russians will be marching down the Champs-Élysées. The Champs-Élysées! A disgrace. A glorious age of peace, undone. Vulgar con-artist delusions. Unfathomable vanity and ignorance. Everything to nothing, for nothing. A complete and utter humiliation. The Russians marching down the Champs-Élysées.

My dad can't make sense of why so many of his colleagues and long-time friends are sympathetic to Trump, why they're still loyal to the Republican Party. Educated, career military officers with decades of service, officers who swore an oath to the Constitution. And yet, so full of excuses for a demagogue who carelessly flouts all the norms of American democracy, a self-styled tyrant, and one who flippantly disrespects the military at that.

Trump scoffs at the very idea of patriotic sacrifice. He openly conspires to overturn the Constitution. Shouldn't they all be united in disgust? Did their oaths mean nothing? My dad starts to see a new immediacy in the Civil War, the dilemma that officers faced as their home states seceded from the Union. Officers who all fought together against the Mexicans and the Indians. Trump is the Confederacy, the dissolution of the Union, the reactionary coup against the democratic order. It all becomes clear after a lifetime of repression. Long-dormant racist attitudes now emerge. The Nazi rally in Charlottesville, where he went to university. A transhistorical connection between the Confederacy and fascism. Yes, sadly many of his lifelong friends would've become Confederates. A present shot-through with the past. First as tragedy, then as farce. The ambient attitude of passive historical reconciliation, something he knows all too well from a Virginian youth and a military career, the homegrown clean Wehrmacht myth—the sainthood of Robert E. Lee, the ubiquity of Confederate monuments, the military bases named after Confederate generals (even mediocre ones—Fort Bragg?), the popular idea that the Confederate army was simply "better" in every way, that it fought with gentility against an extraordinarily cruel and inhuman Union army, not to mention the obvious whitewashing of racism—all a collaborationist lie. There was never any honor in the cause, there was never any noble sacrifice, just apocalyptic treason. There is nothing to celebrate in his own Confederate ancestry. The South had brought about its own ruin—the complete annihilation of Richmond, Atlanta, Charleston, and so on—all for the arrogance of its ghoulish slave-owning class. This man had even once named a dog after Pierre Gustave Toutant-Beauregard. That was a more naïve time. Now he realizes everything must be renamed. Jefferson Davis Highway might as well be Trump Highway. As he goes on, I hear melancholy echoes of the interminable arguments with his colleagues. "You know, Grant was never really the 'butcher' they all say he was…"

I put the copyediting skills from my day job to use with pro-bono revisions to an article my dad wrote for a technical defense industry magazine about the strategic importance of selling Tomahawk cruise missiles to the Japanese military.

***

In DC, my studies of the incels could be more legible if I didn't try to be a poet. Trying to be a psychoanalyst sort of straddles the line. The unconscious is structured like a language. The psychoanalyst can play a sort of avant-garde literary critic, but can also play a cop. Here, the cop wins. Literal terrorism is what counts, not so much the metaphorical, poetic kind. I need to be a counterterrorism expert. The incel as a subset of the lone-wolf terrorist paradigm. A form of asymmetric warfare. A threat to national security. I am a Fellow at the Institute for the Studies of Virginity. Kissless and handholdless wonk. Incelligence operative. The Russians are running jouissance-interference operations in the incel forums, sowing doubt in Western liberal democratic norms and institutions. My arch-rival is the FSB's Fyodor Dostoevsky. I need to get on the deradicalization grift. I need to cooperate with partners and international organizations to leverage the full potential of each stakeholder in the global counter-incel effort. INCELOPS. Senior Researcher of Not Getting Pussy Committee on Coolness Research. Institute for the Defense of Nice Guys. Buy a Wheelchair to Pick Up Women Game Theorist. Clitoris Denialism Countersignaling Guru. Penis Theorist. The threat of terrorism lurks in the absences that characterize human sexuality at its most essential. Yes, everywhere. The erotic metaphysics of alienation. Lots of funding will be needed. An extensive Borgesian database of incel radicalization—vaster than all existing human knowledge and constructed in collaboration with hundreds of researchers from dozens of allied nations —will list the forms of inceldom, both empirically-observed and theoretical, only some of which I repeat here: acnecel, americel, arabcel, aristocel, artcel, autistcel, aryancel, baldcel, blackcel, bincel, bourgcel, chadcel, christocel, clergycel, cuckcel, currycel, cybercel, denialcel, elbowcel, emcel, escortcel, ethnicel, eyecel, femcel, framecel, gaycel, geocel, gooncel, gymcel, haircel, hitlercel, jewcel, lesbocel, litcel, mentalcel, muslimcel, nearcel, NEETcel, noncel, nosecel, nymphocel, oldcel, opcel, peniscel, permacel, persocel, poorcel, prolecel, protocel, quasicel, queercel, quirkcel, rainbowcel, ricecel, roidcel, semicel, skinnycel, smallcel, standardcel, stoicel, stuttercel, sunandsteelcel, tradcel, transcel, truecel, turkcel, uglycel, undergroundcel, whitecel, workcel, wristcel, yellowcel, youngcel, zencel...

Pareidolia

Stephanie Yue Duhem

would be a beautiful name for a girl.

Instead, it's blotches of brown on toast
or whorls in a marble shower.

Three tree gnarls in close proximity.
Five gobs of fat in stew.

Snapdragon pods or a graveyard of skulls.
Soap suds or a choir of yawns.

Not to mention the furrowed brow
of a crumpled towel on the floor—

in all these contours,
my love,
I have seen you before.

In a tile
in a tower
that reaches up
like a white and slender arm.

Ruben

Alex Perez

I don't know how he got my number, but five years after I'd last seen him, I got a call from Ruben. I was in bed with a girl who at the time I thought to be the one, but who only turned out to be one of the many I ran off. I'd been trying to escape Miami and what I called my dirty Hispanic nature, but when I saw that infamous 305, I automatically picked up.

"Remember me?" he said.

I wish I could say that I didn't, but I was immediately taken back to the day he'd sold my brother and me the M80s.

"Ruben?" I said.

"I fucked up," he said. "I don't know why I called, probably because you were supposed to be smart or some shit, but I had to tell someone."

I sat up in bed, as did the white girl of my dreams. I didn't want to know what Ruben had done, because I knew he was capable of anything, murder—rape—genocide, but I knew he was going to tell me anyway.

"What did you do, Ruben?"

"I was always a piece of shit, wasn't I?" he said.

The truth was, when I'd known him, I thought Ruben to be one of the great pieces of shit of all time, but after spending a semester with the proper kind of people, the people who had all the right ideas and excellent personal style and voted for the correct politicians, it had occurred to me that Ruben was one of the great men. He might've been a savage, and perhaps, as he had said, a piece of shit, but he was someone who was unable to pretend—unlike me, one of the great pretenders of all time.

"When I knew you, Ruben," I said, "you were the real deal. Whatever you did, and I don't care what it is, that's the way I'll always think of you. I'll never forget the night of the acid bomb, one of the great nights of my life. These people here, where I'm at right now, they wouldn't believe a guy like you exists even if I told them. You're better than all of them, Ruben, certainly better than me. Trust me when I tell you that no matter what you did, it's no worse than what I've done."

"What the fuck did you do?" Ruben said. "You kill a motherfucker?"

I told him in the only way I knew he'd understand, the only way that truly mattered anyway.

"I turned into a pussy. I was a coward when you knew me, no doubt about it, but I wasn't a pussy yet."

The girl next to me, who had only ever heard me speak of obscure French writers and coma-inducing Norwegian films, gasped and scooted away from me.

"Just stop being a pussy," Ruben said.

"I don't know how," I said. "Can you believe I'm wearing a beret now?"

"What the fuck is that?"

"It's a little French hat pussies wear."

"The first thing you need to do is burn that hat," Ruben said. "You burn that shit and then you start wearing a big ass gold chain. You remember the chain I used to wear?"

How could I forget Ruben's gold chain? He tried to put it on me once, but I was so afraid the massive chain would send me to the ground that I ran off before he could do it. If only I had worn the chain and some of Ruben's honesty and vitality and balls had rubbed off on me.

"It was the best gold chain I'd ever seen," I said.

"You can have it," Ruben said, "as long as you answer one question."

The girl next to me stood up and put on a Bob Dylan record—*John Wesley Harding*—and started dancing what she probably thought was some sexy hippie dance. She was trying to summon me back, I think, to remind me that I had risen from the urban streets of my youth and was no longer a dirty Cuban, but ten thousand of her couldn't defeat a single Ruben.

"Ask me," I said.

"I'm on the run," Ruben said. "Should I turn myself in or keep running?"

The right thing to do was to tell him to turn himself in, that no matter what he'd done he could get past it. The girl kept dancing her rhythm-less dance, and Dylan, like always, just wouldn't shut the fuck up. This is where you ended up, I thought, if you always did the right thing.

"Whatever you do," I said, "you keep running. Don't let these motherfuckers catch you."

Ruben didn't say anything for a few seconds, but then he laughed the same laugh he'd laughed the night he blew up the acid bomb.

"They'll never catch me," he said. "I'm Ruben."

"Yes, you are," I said. "You're fucking Ruben."

"And no friend of mine is a pussy," he said.

Then Ruben hung up.

I faced the girl, who had stopped dancing and was now just looking at me as if I was some kind of monster.

"Who was that?" she said.

"That's the guy, who, by himself, would take over this town if he wanted to. He'd make everyone here his bitch. He'd teach classes on how to make acid bombs and how to get strippers to suck you off on the cheap. He'd fuck every girl, and no one, absolutely no one, would be able to stop him."

"You know him?" she said.

"Intimately."

"What did he do?"

I stood up and walked over to her, this perfectly lovely, tasteful girl I no longer wanted anything to do with.

"From the sounds of it, if I had to guess, I'd say murder, or at the very least, manslaughter."

She shut the music off and Dylan finally went quiet.

"And you told him to run," she said.

I inched closer and put my hands on her hips.

"Why don't you twerk a little bit?" I said.

"I don't know what that means," she said.

"You know, drop it like it's hot. Put some ass into it."

She shook her head.

"I hope he runs all the way over here so I can harbor him. We can harbor a criminal together. Wouldn't that be an interesting story you can tell your friends when you go back to New York on break?"

"I need to go," she said.

I released her and stepped aside.

"More room for Ruben and me," I said.

She walked past me and headed to the door, grabbing the handle. She looked at me and shook her head.

"This is very unlike you," she said. "You're acting like an animal."

I can't tell you why I did what I did next, only that it came from deep inside me and I was powerless to hold it in. I barked at my girlfriend. She made a face one makes, I guess, when a person barks at them, a face so hilarious that I could only bark again. She ran out of the apartment, leaving the door open. I kept barking like some mangy mutt. I wanted that entire town to hear me barking. I wanted them to know who I was and what I was and that I was nothing like them. I barked and barked and stomped on the beret and did a couple of crotch chops and barked and barked and when I finally went quiet, for the first time in my life, I knew who I was.

Brainscreen

August Lamm

I decide to join the park athletes and run laps around the duck pond. I don't have the proper gear, just a pair of casual sneakers, a sweatshirt, and some linen pajama bottoms. I'm not trying to set any records here. I think about the sugar daddy in his eighties who said he was uncertain as to whether he could still get erections, but that it didn't matter because he *wasn't practicing for the sex olympics*. I am also not practicing for the sex olympics, nor even the regular olympics nor a marathon nor a 10k nor even a 5k. I have doubts about my ability to run a single k. My aim with running is to prevent, or at least delay, the mental breakdown I can feel building in my chest like a sneeze.

I slip a house key into my sock and step out the door, jogging down the steps and out onto the street. What even is a *breakdown*, really? Where is the line between lapse and collapse? It's extremely cold and I don't have gloves. Isn't everyone always in the process of falling apart, at least in some sense? It's not actually that cold, I've just gotten soft in England. Maybe a breakdown is not the breaking down itself, but the failure to build things up again. Everyone breaks down. Show me a person and I'll show you a breakdown in progress, the question is what stage. The weather here is awful precisely because it's never awful enough, it's always just a little bit awful. Bearable. At least have the decency to freeze my tits off if you're going to be cold. Who is *you*? A real breakdown would be: slipping on the metaphorical sidewalk and then, instead of dusting yourself off and insisting you're fine, instead of mending your clothes and cleaning your wounds, instead of smiling reassuringly at the crowd of concerned onlookers, you just lie there on the sidewalk looking miserable, refusing to help yourself, refusing to reassure anyone, until eventually you begin to feel at home there, thinking of your past self as this disingenuously upright person, walking around all normal when the whole time, deep down, you were this sidewalk person, so only now are you embodying your true self, and you stay there for a long time, and then it gets kind of boring and you try to stand up again, only to find that your legs do not work anymore. Really, all I can think about right now is my legs. They hurt. I keep going, trotting along. *I am not practicing for the sex olympics.* I am trying to break my body down. *Breakdown.* I am trying to make myself so physically uncomfortable that my mind becomes irrelevant and my body becomes this rusted, limping, breathless piece of machinery, dragging itself along the running path.

In the park, everyone is wearing skin-tight technical gear composed of mesh and reflective material. Everyone has headphones, too. I imagine them listening to high-BPM dance tracks, or podcasts with celebrity hosts, or audiobooks about maximizing investment returns and cultivating a growth mindset. It's moments like these that make me really crave a smartphone, make me want one so badly that I cease to perceive the ducks and the fountains and my fellow athletes. A browser pops up on my brainscreen and mentally I type into the search bar, *used iphone,* and then I look through the offers and think, *Hey, not actually that expensive, especially if it's an older model,* and then I think of strategies to prevent my total technological dependence this time around, strategies for keeping one foot planted firmly in real life, though I know once I get a phone I will surrender to it the majority of my attention and autonomy, because I'm too weak, because I'm a fundamentally weak person, because there's no world in which I find a way to do tech, or really anything, in moderation.

Maybe I could buy a phone but keep it turned off, using it only in case of emergency. This is addict thinking: I know very well I'll never turn the phone off. I'll spend the first few weeks with it in bed, catching up on screentime, downloading things and swiping around and making new accounts and taking photos and typing out little notes and watching videos and waiting for people to write me back. For that sweet, tortured, bedridden chapter, before I inevitably sell the phone, I will outsource my capacity for thought to a little screen that flattens and constrains the dimensions of my mind. Only in sleep will my mind grow unchecked, out of bounds. I will be sure to trim it back, to look at the screen, as soon as I wake.

I am still running even though every part of me, every organ, every limb, every joint and tendon, every cell is telling me to stop. My body is getting so loud that I can't even hear my thoughts anymore, which was kind of the goal but also freaks me out. My mind is too quiet now. I get lonely and slow to a walk.

Screens are what we turn to when we no longer want to exist. Maybe I no longer want to exist. Is existence doing me any good these days? *It's still better than the alternative*, I say to myself automatically, meaning death, which admittedly I know very little about but which sounds super scary. I start running again so I don't have to think about death. I am still on my first lap around the pond. The burning in my lungs begins to erase my thoughts again, the way a smartphone erases thoughts, or the way fire eats up a piece of paper. This is a satisfying image: typewritten words fading into ash. I'm kind of into running now. I could be a runner. I try to think about death again and I can't, the thought dissolves in the lung blaze. If I could just remain forever in this perfect zone of distracting yet survivable pain, I'd be totally set. If I could just run and run, right until the moment my dad dies, I'd be in great shape for the funeral, physically and emotionally. But I can't keep running because I have work to do. I really need to get back to work. Jesus, I really have to send those emails. What is wrong with me? I could easily take care of it today, ready or not. I could take care of it the moment I get home, harness these exercise endorphins to overcome my own indolence. I could get up off the sidewalk. I could unbreak. *Hi, first off, I'm so sorry for the delay*, I type on my brainscreen. *I've been in the U.S. taking care of my father for the past month*. Technically, I only visited for a week, but the week did occur in the past month, and besides, there's no universally accepted definition of *for the past month*. Language is a living entity, continually evolving to suit new purposes. Language is only meaningful insofar as it serves us. Serves me. *I just got back to London this week and I'm catching up on work, so you should expect an update in the next week or so*. I have always been partial towards loose timeframes like this rather than concrete deadlines, although on second thought, maybe a concrete deadline is exactly what I need. *I'll have the piece done by January 15th*, I type mentally. But that doesn't sound like something I would say. In fact, I'm not sure I've ever invoked a future date in an email. I only use dates retroactively, to describe things I've already done, the past being one thing I can't possibly fuck up.

I reach my house. I remove my shoes and enter my bedroom. There is no reason I cannot send the emails now. *What a day I've had.* All the necessary tools are at my disposal. *I've been feeling a lot, processing those emotions.* I am fully available, fully competent, ready to begin. *I am getting evicted.* I am still technically on the lease. *I am crying.* I can write an email while crying. *I need to be kind to myself.* I need to crack down. *I need to get out of these wet clothes first, put my shoes on the radiator to dry.* The computer doesn't care about my physical state. The computer just wants to be used. *I just want to relax, get into bed, read a book.*

If I could send even one email tonight, then tomorrow I'd wake up and feel encouraged by that modest start, and in the morning I'd set a timer for thirty minutes and send as many emails as possible, and then I would go for a walk. *I don't need to send an email to earn a walk.* I would stop at a bookstore and not buy anything because I have no money. *It's not about the money right now.* I would read the first few pages of some new releases, and then I would walk back out into the world, feeling a part of the creative sector, feeling in the know, and I would pine for the stick-legged whippets and Italian greyhounds trotting along in their winter coats. *I've got enough to handle without a dog.* I would look at the blotched cheeks of the babies in strollers. I don't even want kids. I would look at the cashmere-topped heads in red and green and navy and lavender, and I would know for certain that this life of purebred dogs and bundled babies and natural fibers would be waiting for me someday, so long as I kept on answering emails. *Go to bed. Don't open the computer.*

When I open the computer, there's a missed video call from my father's phone. My father can't operate a phone, so it must be his girlfriend, or a nurse. For a moment I feel certain that my father has died, then I feel certain that he's alive because why would anyone do a video call to break that sort of news? Surely they would opt for the more traditional, more understated audio route. But then again, they might have hit the wrong button. Maybe they didn't mean to call me at all. That would be ideal. It's late and I've been crying and all I want is to feel bad for myself— difficult to do when faced with a dying man. I hesitate then click the audio icon. The ringtone begins. I wish for him not to answer, the way I sometimes wish for him not to wake up.

Hello, who am I speaking to? The voice is not my father's. It's a man's voice but it's clear, intelligible.

Yes, hi, I'm looking for my father.

One moment. There is shuffling and murmuring, and I can tell that the phone has been handed to my father, but not put on speaker, which means my father will have to hold it to his face and aim for the microphone, which he always finds difficult, but now the phone is already in my father's hands and I can't ask my father to put it on speaker because he doesn't know how to do that, and he would probably just end the call accidentally. I hope the other man has gone away. I don't like the idea of someone hearing even one side of the conversation.

Hi, dad?

Hello? Hello? Can you hear me?

Yes, dad, it's me.

My daughter.

How are you doing? I ask.

Well, I have a sore throat, he says. *And my feet aren't working,* he adds. *And it's black outside.*

How long have you had the sore throat? I ask, relieved at the introduction of a clear conversational direction.

A few weeks now.

I was with you last week though, I say, not knowing why I bother contradicting him. *I was there and you didn't have a sore throat.*

No, it was a while ago that you were here.

Okay, I relent. *Have you spoken to the doctor?*

The doctor's coming tomorrow, he says. I am not sure whether to trust this. It doesn't affect me whether or not the doctor is real. Still, I feel the need to establish my father's lucidity before continuing the conversation, to establish which version of him I'm speaking to, and how my words will be received, and whether they'll be retained. It occurs to me that the more demented he is, the less nervous I am.

There is a long pause during which I can hear his labored breathing —it sounds like he's jogging underwater—and all I can think to say is, *Your breathing doesn't sound great, either.*

It's the sore throat, he says.

Right, I say. I can't tell which one of us is being stupid. I consider asking him if he's had any visitors recently, but if he hasn't had visitors, or can't remember having them, it'll be depressing to talk about. *Are you feeling settled there now? Are you liking it?*

Settled where? he asks. I hesitate over the wording. I don't want to be the one to remind him where he lives, just in case he's been able to imagine himself elsewhere.

You know? I say, but he still doesn't seem to know. *You got transported last week?*

He thinks for a minute, breathing heavily, then says: *I'd really like to get back on my feet.*

Just keep doing your exercises, I say. *You're seeing the physical therapist?*

Oh, sure, he says, and it's not clear if he's joking or serious or has any idea what we're talking about. *It's black outside.* I imagine him trying to look out the window. *I haven't even had my breakfast and I'm already drowsy.*

I think it's about seven in the evening there, I say. *And almost midnight here in London.* I'm hoping this will bring the conversation to a natural conclusion. There is another pause, much longer than I am comfortable with, but no words come to me, I forget what we're supposed to be talking about, what our relationship is supposed to be, how long we've been on the phone, and I wonder if this is what it's like to be him, lost, all the time. Is it contagious? Have I entered into his state willingly, to make him feel less alone? I hear only his breath on the line. There is nothing to say. He can't read anymore and the TV in his room is broken so I can't ask which media he's been consuming. I can't mention his death because he doesn't believe he will die, nor can I mention his recovery because I don't believe he will recover.

I'm an awful father, he says, and I am grateful not to be on video.

What do you mean? I ask.

I get so tired every time you call me. I want to tell him that this is the only time I've called, that in the days since I left I've been caught up in a series of minor dramas, that I've engineered these dramas to avoid thinking about him, and that he always finds a way in anyway. Mostly, I want to tell him that he's right, he was an awful father, he is an awful father, he's awful for his absence and awful for his presence, and I would have been better off if he'd left cleanly and permanently, rather than feeding me slivers of himself at erratic intervals over the years, insisting that these pale wafers of patrimony were the body, the flesh of love.

That's alright, Dad. I'm tired, too.

I think I'll go to sleep now, he says.

I can hear him put the phone down on the bed, the friction of sheets against the microphone, and then the phone seems to settle, and I can hear his breathing, and I know that I can keep listening as long as I like, can get into my bed right now and drift off to the sound of my father's sleep, but I also know I wouldn't be able to drift off because I would be listening for a change, for a slowing or quickening or stopping, and I don't want to fear that moment, and I don't want to hope for it either, so I end the call.

House of Hope

August Lamm

I was in New Haven, walking back from the hospital to my father's apartment. This particular street had always felt a bit risky to me. I knew it was problematic to think this way, to feel afraid of a street, but still I spent the whole walk thinking about getting killed, hating myself for thinking it, and almost wanting to get killed, either to justify my fears or get them to stop. I did my best not to seem afraid, so the potential killers would perceive me as inoffensive, and then decide not to kill me. There were a few halfway houses along the way, and in front of one of them was a group smoking and chatting. They all went quiet as I passed, then picked up the conversation once I was further down the block. They were probably going to kill me. They were probably talking about movies or the internet. I kept my head down, a posture of deference or defense, none of us could be certain.

My father's building was fifteen stories tall. He and his partner lived on the seventh floor. I rarely took elevators wherever I went. I despised the shape of my body and, like many women, felt certain that I was just one minor lifestyle change away from total self-acceptance.

The building itself was irredeemably ugly, with brown metal siding stuck to an arbitrary grid of brick and concrete. It was not the sort of building you'd look at twice, so I never remembered much about its exterior. I signed in with the doorman and marched up the six flights of stairs, taking each step in time with the syllables of my mental mantra: I-want-to-kill-my-self. I am not sure when or why this mantra emerged, but it likely had to do with the fact that there were exactly six steps between each landing, and that I wanted to kill myself.

I reached the apartment door and tried the handle. It was unlocked. I entered and closed the door behind me. The apartment smelled like a dusty sunbeam, cut with the sour tang of old piss. It was winter and the windows were almost always closed. I assumed a posture that assured my audience I had definitely not been contemplating suicide on the walk home. My father didn't live here anymore; it was just his partner, Marina, and all his belongings. If he'd been here and not in the hospital, I would've opened the door to a phlegmy throat-clearing sound, which would've erupted into a coughing fit, which would've subsided, ending with a deep, patrician sigh. Finally there would've been the soft crinkle of a newspaper laid down on a tablecloth. And then, *My daughter*. He always greeted me as though I had just shown up in the middle of the night, in a record-breaking snowstorm, twenty years after the last time we'd seen each other. In a sense, this was the general tone of our relationship: astonishment that we had any relationship at all. I had not grown up with him. He had never taken care of me. And yet here I was, taking care of him, enacting a filial duty neither of us really believed was mine.

***

I removed my shoes slowly, then stood in the hall in my socks. I could take as long as I needed to acclimate upon arrival because Marina was partially deaf and couldn't hear the door. I took stock of my physical state. I was starving. I tried to calculate what time it was in London, to figure out what meal this would be, or if my alternate London self was already asleep. I couldn't do the math. My brain was like one of those little paper cones dispensed at water coolers: it could only hold so much, and there was always a little trickle leaking out the bottom. I should probably eat. I heard slippered footsteps in the kitchen, then saw Marina's slight frame cross the room. She looked so vulnerable, her back turned to me, still unaware of my presence. *Marina*, I said, and as usual she jumped in shock, then smiled and said, *Oh good, I've just put some chicken salad in the fridge. There's also some chili if you want something hot*. This would be the moment to say I'm vegan. *Good*, I said. I was so two-faced. It seemed like in order to avoid disappointing anyone, I had to lie to everyone. The chicken salad was scrumptious. It had mayo and craisins in it and almost tasted like dessert.

I checked my computer before bed. My flatmate Faith had messaged me.

How's it going over there

it's awful, i couldn't believe how bad he looked
i want to come home already
but obviously i need to be here
i know it's not about me

I imagine it's a lot of pressure, knowing this might be the last time you'll get
with him

brutal

I'm just repeating back what you said a few days ago
Doing the reflecting thing you like

Maybe I should also mention that Faith and I were sleeping
together.

ok, I wrote. *well then i'm brutal*

You are, sometimes
It's weird, I always feel like it's a bit different chatting online with you
Versus real life

different how?

I can't describe it
Maybe it's just cause I don't chat online with a lot of people
In real time like this

I didn't know what she was getting at, and it bothered me. This just felt like the latest in Faith's series of attempts to create emotional distance. But maybe there was also something to it, maybe I was different online, and maybe it was intentional. Now that I thought of it, I did type in lowercase with Faith, and sentence case with my other flatmate, Soren, whom I was also fucking.

can you try describing the difference? I wrote.

I don't know, maybe there's no difference
I was going to say something nice about you

What

That you've got such a distinct personality, it comes through regardless of medium
But then I felt like that was more complimentary than true

why can't it be both
why can't the truth be nice

It can be
I'm just saying it was probably more of a knee-jerk compliment

so i don't have a distinct personality

Ok now you sound just like you do in real life

isn't it like 3 am there

Yep

I hated how our conversations could end like this, tapering off into silence. Was I always just one uninspired message away from being ignored? Maybe Faith wasn't really ignoring me; the conversation had reached a natural conclusion. In a perfect world, everyone would talk to me forever. Or just Faith, maybe. Where did Faith go when we stopped talking? Did she put her phone down? I didn't even have a phone, I'd sold my phone, I'd gone phoneless. I now required a laptop and desktop program and a stable internet connection just to send a message, and still I was a more consistent correspondent than Faith. What was she doing when she didn't reply? Was she messaging more interesting people? Was she making plans with these people? Was she going out to meet them?

She barely ever left the house. She was always online. I mentally replayed all the times I'd come across her in the living room, messaging other girls on dating apps, and it made me want to break my lease.

hey, I wrote a few minutes later. I wanted to make sure Faith was still awake first.

Yes? she replied.

are you still thinking about the michael jackson documentary

Um no not particularly
Why do you ask?

i just thought it was very affecting

You mean effective?

no like it affected me a lot

How

i really connected with michael

He's not even in the film

but he is. his energy is

He was a pedophile

well yeah i'm not apologizing for him

Sometimes when people questioned my morality, I wanted to say something like, *I'm Jewish,* except that there were tons of Jews in the world, it wasn't special, and also I hadn't even been Bat Mitvah'd and I looked fully Caucasian, so my Judaism had literally never affected me except for this one time (I remember it so clearly) when a friend made a weird comment about being nervous around the Orthodox people in her neighborhood. And I was no better than her, no less afraid of ethnic minorities in my own neighborhood. I also wanted to say something like, **I'm disabled,** but I didn't know if that was supposed to mean, *I'm the real victim here,* or else, *The pain makes it hard for me to be a good person so I get a free pass.* I decided against invoking either of these identities in our chat about Michael Jackson.

i just think michael was a severely damaged person, I wrote to Faith.

Yes, she replied. I could feel her wanting to go to bed, trying to wrap up our conversation and log off. I could feel it all just through that one little word, *yes.*

weirdly i could relate to the plastic surgery stuff, I wrote
the urge to change / reduce yourself

Good thing you're already extremely pale

i'm being serious here

ok sorry i just don't know what you're getting at
i'm really tired

What was I getting at? Maybe what I was trying to do, in recalling the film, was to recall the evening we'd watched the film, to ask Faith: *Why didn't you let me sit near you?* Or really, to ask: *Why didn't you come to my room afterward?* But Soren had come to my room. Did I want her to usurp Soren, to kick him out and replace him in my memory? Did I want her to join us? Did I want her to walk in on us and for everything to fall apart? I once read this dating advice column where a woman wrote in to say that she'd been seeing two guys, and she liked them both a lot, and the time had come to choose which one to pursue more seriously. The columnist told her, *If you're so torn between them that you're writing to an advice columnist, neither is right.* I hated that advice. If, for example, I received twice the food I'd ordered at a restaurant, would I throw both in the trash, and insist that they both be included on the bill? No, I'd enjoy my gigantic meal and blame the mistake on someone else. *Neither is right.* But what if both were right? Or what if both were half right, and together they added up to one right? *Neither is right.* The advice did not sit well with me. And yet, years after reading it in some outdated fashion magazine in a doctor's office, I still thought about it all the time.

***

The bedroom I slept in at Marina's apartment was my dad's old bedroom. Years earlier, Marina had commandeered the guest room in order to escape my father's snoring and hourly piss breaks. I thought it might be weird sleeping in my dad's bed, but I didn't feel much of anything once I was there, maybe because I was so tired. I forced myself to stay awake until a normal bedtime, in order to get ahead of the jet lag. I opened a document on my computer and wrote out a list of all the different bedrooms I'd had in the past few years. It was a surprisingly difficult task, especially with a water-cone brain. I counted twenty before falling asleep at eleven. I woke about a dozen times in the night before finally getting out of bed at four in the morning. Nothing made sense. The darkness was infinite, the sun a theoretical concept, the coffee machine too complicated for me to figure out. *Maybe it'll be fine*, I thought. *Maybe it's a borderline case.* I dug through the pantry for tea and found an old bag of Earl Grey wrapped in a skein of moth webbing, dotted with tiny eggs. The teabag itself was safely sealed. I microwaved a mug of water and thought about the scorn I'd incurred in London for doing this, as though microwaved water was somehow different from kettle-boiled water. I drank the tea without milk because there was only dairy milk and I was vegan again.

I went back to the pantry looking for cereal, and found something even better: a canister of oats. If I could only eat one food for the rest of my life, it would be oatmeal. Actually, I would happily subsist exclusively on oatmeal, if only it were nutritionally complete. I had previously contemplated—and, for brief spells, actually attempted—eating oatmeal for three meals a day, supplementing it with vitamins. These were not my healthiest phases, my body seeming to take on the properties of oatmeal, becoming lumpen and colorless, losing its vitality, its spice. Despite having tested this lifestyle and deemed it unsustainable, I still struggled with the temptation at every mealtime to microwave a bowl of oats. Nothing else was so pleasing to my senses, so warm and wet and soft and comforting. Oatmeal was like an oral blanket. I wanted oats and only oats. All the other foods I ate—all the vegetables, even the pastries and desserts—seemed like an infidelity.

I put some oats into a bowl then poured tap water over them. I liked my oats watery, extremely watery. In fact, I probably liked my oats more watery than anyone else on the planet. I would've bet money on that. My preferred ratio was three parts water to one part oats, so that the final product was just a smooth gelatinous fluid studded with the occasional flake of oat. I loved oat water so much. It was like a pacifier to me. No matter what was going on in my life, how tired or anxious or depressed I felt, no matter how lonely or lovesick or guilty, for the five minutes it took to slurp up my oat glue, I was alright. If I needed serious pacifying, I might extend the cooking process to include multiple stages of microwaving, stirring, letting it soak, then microwaving again, stirring again, and letting it cool down so I could eat it without burning my tongue. At certain difficult junctures in my life, the oatmeal ritual had stretched out to over an hour—and that was just the time it took to prepare one bowl, one meal. The maximum number of oatmeal bowls I had consumed in a day was four. The minimum was one. So to find a canister of oats in Marina's cupboard was to find a way forward, a way through the existential dread and material discomfort involved in a deathbed pilgrimage. To find a canister of oats was to find hope.

One time, Soren and I got curious and did a Google search for Connecticut. We were in the kitchen. I read the results aloud while he washed a pan. I remember finding this mention of an early settlement called the *House of Hope*—some sort of Dutch trading post—and it was described as *small and short-lived*. When I read that line, I laughed so hard I almost threw up. Soren laughed a bit too, but indulgently, compliantly, and he continued washing the pan as I wore myself out in a fit of hilarity. *Small and short-lived*, I kept screaming. *The House of Hope was small and short-lived.* I couldn't stop repeating the line. I couldn't believe how perfect it was.

Baseball Sonnet

Tom Will

Baseball movies keeping score
In their own way stations of the cross
Inside a cinema batting at the drapes
The screen as well ignominious, consider
Swinging a bat in a basement batting cage
The cinderblock cool bat
This infamous gibbet the chainlink gate
Our marriage bed the bird rattling fence
The vodka on the jersey neck
The coke can in the street
The kicking of a lonely gravel stone
The joggers kicking at long life
The golf cart on the baseball field
The ashes scattering on the reef

Frenzy Without Feeling

Chris R. Morgan

The Gen X nature is Janus-faced. It sees no contradiction in practicing ethics of the highest possible standard while exalting morals at the lowest reachable nadir. In the mid-1990s it was not atypical to be handed an Amnesty International leaflet by someone in a Budd Dwyer t-shirt. A Jim Rose Circus performer could make a pin cushion out of his testicles while flanked by a Planned Parenthood tent and Shaolin monks. This nature was harmonious insofar as it broke decidedly with natures that preceded it. It broke with the socially mandated sentimentality of American culture just as it broke with the inherited sanctimony of their parents and grandparents. The Gen X nature reflected the real conditions of the world as Gen Xers saw it, leaving them to set their own moral boundaries and to pick their own ethical battles.

If Steve Albini was not the most ideal specimen of that nature, he was the most enthusiastic. Few of his contemporaries were more jealous of their personal integrity, and few were more vociferous in living it out with greatest consistency. In the wake of his death much has been said of his advocacy for the independence of the artist while being able to accept the costs that came with it. He refused lucrative royalty opportunities as an in-demand record engineer (he disapproved of "producer," even as people still described him as such). He worked with the most famous and the most obscure and saw no difference between them. He warned in the most explicit terms of the impossible tradeoffs artists would be faced with if they crossed into the major label industry—though most preferred to learn the hard way. Touch and Go Records is one of the few labels from the indie golden age to have survived and thrived from its inception, and Albini remained loyal to it on both sides of the soundboard.

But much will also be said of personal antics that knew no ceiling of offense. His paper trail of grossly unsublimated zine rants will be pored over where found. His friendships with unsavory characters like Peter

Sotos will be referenced again and again. People will retch anew at his violently unpleasant music released under the most shamelessly baiting band names. This ascetic ethicist was also an exquisite sadist. He was not above trashing bands he worked with (the Pixies most famously), and he loved a sick joke (the original cover art for Big Black's *Headache* EP was a crime scene photo of a shotgun suicide). The man who took pains to protect people from economic and artistic exploitation fully exploited the rot and savagery of humanity for his own ends and amusement. He offered a taste of cultural prestige that was cheap in more ways than one.

An ethicist may adopt sadism in any condition. Both modes seek a level of purity that most people find impossible to even imagine. It may be, however, that the dual purity Albini embodied and impressed upon an entire culture was well suited to the moment of its appearance. Everyone, myself included, knew his work before they knew his name. Everyone heard at least one song off of *In Utero* and many others will vehemently deny—or perversely valorize—their ownership of *Razorblade Suitcase*. But some wanted to pursue that purity a little further than the multitude. I never met Steve Albini, nor do I regret it. I mourn him within reason, as someone who served his purpose.

I bought Big Black's *Songs About Fucking* around 1999 or 2000. I was 15 years old, and on the surface it seems like the very object that would magnetize the hard-earned income of any 15-year-old male. Yet this was hardly the case. At that time parents were still blaming Marilyn Manson and Fred Durst for the ills of the world. I don't even think it had a "parental advisory" label. My classmates were no wiser. If they were aware of the band they were not especially moved by them. I discovered the band through my own pursuits; I acquired the record based on my own judgment, easily enough done as Borders carried it and my parents exerted no control over what I consumed. Moreover, I purchased it based entirely upon the description of its sound. It was "industrial," an aesthetic from which I still held out hope for some satisfaction. Interest was piqued even as expectations were middling.

My listening experience came over me in waves. The first wave was aesthetic. Once the prurience wore off (quickly, as none of the songs were actually about fucking) I could appreciate how well-made an album it was. Albini's songwriting prowess is little spoken of. He's an idiosyncratic yet highly controlled and versatile guitarist. I don't consider Big Black's first full-length *Atomizer* the masterpiece others do, but it is a kind of monument to how one can adhere to and totally undermine pop songwriting. This strength (to which disenchanted synth-pop artist and fellow Chicagoan Al Jourgensen was paying very close attention) came out of the rigorous grooves of its rhythm section. The band famously used a Roland drum machine that disciplined the throbbing of Dave Riley's bass. The result made Big Black the sociopath's new wave band; songs like "Kerosene" and "Fists of Love" are club bangers provided that club has a lot of consensual harm happening around it.

Songs About Fucking does not lack for grooves but it is much more the guitar record. They come so loud in the mix as to slash right through it. And "slash" is an appropriate word when set against the pummeling preferred by other noise-rock bands like Swans, Unsane, and Killdozer. There is a cold, calculated frenzy being conjured that resists the spiraling regimentation of a typical hardcore mosh pit. They seemed quite menacing in a live setting. Big Black's impact could be as aggressive as their peers' but the intensification of style through craft allowed for sustained absorption of that impact, making quick dispersion both difficult and not very desirable.

The second wave was cultural. *Songs About Fucking* abjures sentiment and resists sentimentalizing after the fact. Its malicious and ugly worldview has not dulled over time. "I'll piss on everything you value," among the few lyrics instantly decipherable, appeared brash and defiant upon first listen and seemed philosophically compelling; 25 years later you may find yourself modifying it for politeness. In New Jersey at the time it was almost a Satanic standpoint. New Jersey was the epicenter of pop punk and whatever wave of emo You and I and Thursday are. It was steeped in the maudlin and self-dramatizing, in provincial trivia and nostalgia for memories as yet unexperienced. New Jersey punk was insular, conservative, and crowded; not an ideal setting for lost people. In isolation I developed a conception of punk that was purer, more singular and less amenable to joining, and where style was as much a show of self-control as self-expression. I rebelled against punk by arriving at its essence.

There is no achievement in that. Finding an essence can easily be conflated with finding an answer. *Songs About Fucking* escaped being a totem of controversy only to become a token of refinement. The quality of its sound and the intensity of its themes had the effect of lavishing praise upon its listeners simply for being present. That is how the punk in high school becomes the hipster in college. It's the valorization of judgment for its own sake; rendering the work static and the audience stationary to the point of becoming decorative. The life of a hipster is the life of a pinned butterfly. Not that I think less of people for perceiving culture as a source of gratification. If I find my proximity to living death significantly narrowed I have only myself to think less of.

A work is valuable not for the single satisfactory answer it provides but by the many new questions it multiplies, like a low-hanging black cloud that, on closer inspection, is a swarm of flies. It was necessary to disassemble *Songs About Fucking* down to its elements. The value of each part being evaluated with the contours of my own consciousness. At its core, the album gave certain permissions. In the particulars was the affirmative permission: to be rude, to exalt bad behavior, to lash out in any direction. This permission was compelling so long as Gen X remained at the center of the known universe and the ethical-moral equilibrium they propounded didn't balance itself out.

But of course they didn't remain and it did balance out, leaving the more general negative permission: not to express or respect feelings that you don't have, not to revere heroes that don't exist, not to applaud accomplishments that are fraudulent, and to submit all frenzy to the elegance of form. Such a permission is more flexible to your own maturity and to the moral flux. Indeed, if the ethical-moral ratio becomes the reverse of what it was, it may not simply be more attractive, but more powerful. You only need watch your manners.

On Bootstrapping

A. M. Hickman

Twenty pounds of rice is, at the time of this writing, $11.70 at Wal-Mart in Massena, NY. That's less than twelve dollars for 30,000 calories of food. Minimum wage is presently $14.20. This means that within 49 minutes of any form of labor in Upstate New York—a man can secure for himself enough food to survive for about twenty days. The gravity of this simple fact is easy to miss in the hyperabundant atmosphere of present-day America; after all, who wants to eat nothing but rice for twenty days? Quickly, most souls who've been incorporated into the modern American cornucopia will raise their objections to the formulation of working for minimum wage for mere *rice*.

I can make more than minimum wage, might be the first objection. *I hate rice,* might be another, or one might state that *if you lived on only rice you'd become malnourished quickly.* Within the context of the modern-day United States, these are all, of course, totally fair objections. There are very few people in this country—even the very poorest—who are getting excited about securing twenty days' rice in 49 minutes of minimum-wage labor. But on the historical scale of time, this possibility is an extreme anomaly that would seem practically unthinkable in almost any era but our own, especially for commoners and peasants of former eras. That the 49 minutes required to secure three weeks of subsistence calories need not involve physical labor of any kind would seem even stranger to our ancient forefathers. Merely sitting at a desk as a hotel night clerk would count for one's monthly rice—sitting and doing literally nothing at all; even *atrophying from physical inactivity*.

From the vista of the medieval peasant, the galley slave, and the nomadic forager, even the most trivial victories of the postindustrial era are magnified into enormous triumphs. Barring a spectacular catabolic collapse of techno-industrial civilization, hoeing rough rows of dry earth for a bleak harvest is simply not on the menu of possible existential fates for residents of developed nations. We are very obviously living in the remotest fantasies of men and women who lived with a very real and palpable fear of hunger for millennia—whether we feel the full weight of this fact or not. This is even true of our absolute poorest citizens.

The speed with which the wealth of nations has multiplied across the industrial human landscape has been nothing short of breakneck. In only a handful of generations, the threat of starving to death has literally disappeared in the vast majority of the world. In fact, consider that María Brañas Morera is, as of January 2024, the oldest living human being on earth. Her father, Joseph Branyas Julia, was born in Spain in 1877—only two years before Ireland's last major famine in 1879. Indeed, within the span of two human lifetimes, hunger has become an inconvenience in the West—it is no longer even the remotest decision-making factor in how one makes a life for himself. We implicitly understand that no matter how far we fall into the depths of "poverty"—we simply will not starve to death under any realistic circumstances whatsoever.

Perhaps the speed of this change can make it difficult to appreciate what a landmark shift these developments represent in the long story of the human race. The hyperabundance generated by an emergent global system of petroleum-driven technologies in farming, shipping, fertilizer manufacture, and other industries has created a set of circumstances in which the prayerful petition in the Our Father prayer—*give us this day our daily bread*—is more than anything now a vague platitude. This is because hunger is now unknown. The Promethean success of our global agricultural system and its dazzling wealth of fruits is now considered to be a foregone conclusion more than a cause for celebration—it is an untold blessing that is now by and large taken for granted.

In fact, this hyperabundance is not only taken for granted—it is viewed as the fundamental and unspoken "starting point" on which the ambitions of men now rest. In previous eras of human history, one's point of departure in venturing outward to secure the necessities of life was obvious—they began by securing what the body needs for survival. Wheat and firewood, sheaves of reed or shingle for a rainproof roof, milk for breakfast, meat for supper, a blanket for baby, a bucket for water, shoes for walking. Men did not strap themselves into recliner-like chairs built atop complicated assemblages of machined steel and combusting gasoline to zip madly down the asphalt; they did not careen through a sea of steel vehicles violently slashing across great bridges daily in order to secure their income. Nor did they aspire to hurtle through the air in great tubes of steel to foreign ports where glistening playboys soak in the saccharine delights of tropical havens; they did not wire any amount of their weekly coin to overseas companies in order to receive the chimerical transmissions of eye-numbing color and sordid plot that one gets from the likes of Netflix and the television. To the contrary of all of this, they simply began their travails in the working world with the simple notion that their work ought to yield the basics required for a few human bodies to thrive in a modest home. To these men, twenty pounds of rice or flour was *something to be proud of*.

Now—a man is judged haughtily as a miserable failure if he cannot secure a complicated and expensive washing-machine or an automobile. If he by his own volition chooses not to procure these machines at virtually any cost to his own health, life, or sanity—he is condemned as a crank and given bleak warnings about his foolish behavior. The mechanism of social control feels, from the perspective of a young man on the cusp of entering the workforce—nearly total. In the Land of the Free, one must pay outrageous mortgages for suburban homes in top-ten regions; one must have an automobile and refrigerator and an electronic oil furnace and an expensive, glimmering piece of glass on which he can constantly have his focus diverted towards the internet.

If he fails in this, he is bitterly reprimanded and cursed—constantly told that he will never find a wife who'll tolerate such an obscure and difficult lifestyle, constantly chided about how *essential* these utterly newfangled inventions are to what most consider to be a **basic** style of living. Friendships strain for the man who deviates even slightly from these social prescriptions—and in some cases, government agencies intervene in his life, condemning his home or even abducting his children merely for the crime of living as all men did until 1959.

And yet by the same token the man is often exhorted to think of his forefathers and to regard them with great esteem—the pioneers and settlers and magnates of industry, all of whom endured countless hardships and came from nothing. The grandfatherly tavern character speaks boastfully of his days as a schoolboy, of walking to school and milking the cow and awakening to find his water-glass frozen solid. As he relates his former life as a historically normal human being, he does so wistfully—wondering what the hell went wrong with "people these days."

Perhaps I would do well to posit the possibility that hippy-dippy practitioners of "going green" and hard-nosed right-wingers who speak admiringly of those who "pull themselves up by their bootstraps" have more in common than either of them imagine. While I myself cannot affix myself to either of these ideologies—not squarely and completely, at least —I can raise my hand as a man who has lived in ways that would appeal to both camps. My "carbon footprint" matched that of an Ethiopian when I lived at a squatter encampment in the desert and hitchhiked out to the California Coast, dining on dumpstered food as a wandering vagrant— and my bootstraps were pulled tight when I joined the military and bought myself my first house at the age of twenty-eight. In relating the various tales that comprise my own biography, I find that many of them have as much appeal to off-grid, armed-to-the-teeth survivalists as they do to ecologically-conscious Yogis. Above all, I reckon my own philosophy on things has the most in common with those of our great-great-grandfathers—who settled the rough North American hinterlands and built the world we now live in.

What is needed – what I have written, and of which these words are planned as the introduction – is a book to detail that philosophy—which can only be properly expressed by offering the practical knowhow of rough sleeping, vagabond traveling, clandestine cabin construction, survival, and the process by which a penniless man can improve his circumstances almost solely by his own wits. If one begins from the perspective of the homeless man enduring a condition of extreme impecunity in any era—when he eventually forces his way up and into permanent quarters, regular income commensurate with his needs, and property ownership, his philosophy will be born not of what is socially normal but of whatever he found to be truly necessary for a worthwhile human existence. The freedom of the "outsider" allows for an insightful vista on the social norms of the wider society from which he came.

I should make a point of saying that I do not necessarily condemn those who seek to indulge in the hyperabundance of modern-day America and her ways. Whether a man wishes to work his way into princely oblivion— what with expensive automobiles, ATVs, high-rent apartments, or other frivolities—is frankly none of my business. I claim no membership in any ideology that would deprive men of their agency over their circumstances, nor do I believe that simple shame is an effective tool at convincing practitioners of dubious or even worthless social norms. I only wish to highlight that what is now considered "normal" in the developed world is a historical anomaly on a thoroughly unprecedented scale—and that most human beings would benefit from re-orienting their "starting point" towards beginning with what is actually necessary to life, and away from taking what is now normal as a given, or worse still, a right. In fact, I might state as a corollary that the infrastructure on which our hyperabundance rests is fairly fragile—and that it could reach its failure point markedly more easily than most like to imagine.

Ideally, my reflections should prove useful to a wide variety of people— homeless folks with an industrious strain, survivalists and 'preppers', practitioners of "simple living," radical religious conservatives and reactionaries, aspiring vagabonds, impecunious Gypsies, heartland re-settlers, bitterly poor yeomen, nostalgic traditionalists with a proclivity for action, and, lest I should forget to mention them, the millions of completely normal first-world Americans who may get the sneaking sense that their way of life may deserve more scrutiny than it presently gets. This compendium of tips, perspectives, ideas, and philosophical discourses could serve any of the aforementioned with a refreshing bit to contemplate in the event that they voluntarily "simplify" their life or **involuntarily** find themselves falling upon harder-than-expected times. And if nothing else—perhaps the reader will, at a minimum, think differently about the price of rice.

Lessons in Staying Too Long at the Fair

Calla Selicious

On my tenth day in Copenhagen, I decide it is time for Lotte and me to admit that we are tourists by paying a visit to one of the oldest theme parks in the world.

Besides sixty dollars, this endeavor takes a lot of cajoling and a little deception. Lotte's British, so she doesn't really know what a rollercoaster is. She's seen them in films, but she thinks that our chances of dying on one of them are actually high instead of just higher than if we didn't go on one.

Considering her fragile constitution, I decide not to emphasize the fact that this whole slightly increased likelihood of death thing is the foundation of a rollercoaster's appeal, and I answer her questions with as much maternal patience as I can muster.

"Do people die on them," she asks me.

"Only the ones that deserve to," I tell her.

"I had an unkind thought just yesterday," she says.

"Oh, that's fine. Everyone gets one to four per day, depending. Unless it was about me, then you'll die for sure."

"It wasn't until now," she mutters.

Images flash through my mind of spending the rest of our time in this city walking its well-maintained streets, riding its timely trains, and having a single sensible craft cocktail before falling into a restorative eight hours of sleep divided appropriately into REM and non-REM cycles.

The other day, we spoke to a local who told us that he couldn't think of anything he wanted. "More money?" he said, like we were asking him to guess. Then he shrugged: "But I don't really need any."

I come to the grim conclusion that if I do not get to go on this rollercoaster, I am going to have to commit an act of very funny vandalism, so before I speak next I summon all the sincere reassurance I can.

"Seriously, though, you only die if a goose flies straight at your head, and that never happens."

"Except for when it does," she says. I can't argue with that, but I know she's relented.

After I manage to convince Lotte that her head bumping lightly against the side of the seat will not give her cauliflower ear à la UFC fighter, we consider our ride on the Demon to be a great success, so much so that we ride it again, and again, and wander around until dusk falls.

We're about to leave the park when I see the Star Flyer, one of those rides where you're strapped into a chair and spun around in a few serene circles high off the ground. We think it will be nice during the sunset, and we get on line.

Most of the time, life is not so kind as to let us know that we have made a mistake until it has had months to ravage our hearts and minds. This was not one of those times. The Star Flyer, I quickly realize, exists primarily to make the park look cool from afar, and in buying into its spectacle I have become it. The circles I thought so serene from ground level, are, in reality, a feat of g-force so nauseating that I am afraid to open my mouth lest I rain stomach-acid-soaked retribution down on the families below.

"I really cherish our friendship," Lotte wails, clutching my sleeve.

"Shut... the fuck... up," I try to hiss, but it comes out as more of a moan.

"I've truly treasured this time with you," she says, ignoring me.

Something whizzes perilously close to my head. "Is that a fucking goose?"

"Oh," she moans, Britishly. "Oh, how we are but winged fowl upon the wind..."

Something jolts our seat, and, at this point, neither of us bothers to scream. I imagine what it will feel like to die; and we will, unquestionably, die, when in two seconds the chair inevitably detaches from the structure and hurtles to the ground with us in it; there's nothing for us to grab and nothing for us to be cushioned by except bony European children; I smell the sharp emptiness of the clean, cold Danish air, and then I smell the scent of grass mixing with putrid Brooklyn humidity in Prospect Park six summers ago when I sneaked out of my house to meet someone, someone I haven't thought about since and whom I'll probably never speak to again; I smell the eggs I've been frying every morning this week in butter, eating them over a slice of heirloom tomato with salt, eating them after waking up with anxiety about what to do with my day and how I'm going to leave my house with a plan and a bag packed for it so that I don't end up doing one errand and feeling lost, the anxiety I've been waiting months to feel again, that I left New York to feel again because it is the form of anxiety I recognize as ambition, and I smell Lotte's shampoo and though it hasn't happened yet, I remember how in two days she and I will stay up like kids at a sleepover on her last night here and I will let her leave in the middle of the night without saying goodbye because I don't want her to, and I smell the recycled air of the plane I took here and remember how when it shook I felt indifferent to if it would fall, tempted for it to, almost, and I realize I am not indifferent anymore; I am disappointed. Disappointed in a way that I recognize from dreams in which to wake up is to die, and I wait to wake up.

The chair has not detached; the ride has just ended. As we are lowered to the ground, I make a note to myself to stop wanting to amass experiences; it is a trait that rarely serves me well. Then I walk past the ride operator, a woman about my age with her hair in braids and a faded zit above her lip, and I tell her she's beautiful, but only because it's true.

Headwaters

Alice Gribbin

We borrow all the water, return
and take again.
What luxury is anymore
doesn't concern us.
The sovereign clouds, the sovereign streams, give freely.

But observing the heavy boughs
is no longer satisfying.
We want a wakeful beauty,
desiring and subjectless,
from someplace far upstream, before the water gets divided.

The framemakers pound the earth flat only to marvel at its
            flatness, make images of mountains
then declare the mountains static.

No, that
will not do.
Convention says
we dig these
hours, we plant
our facts, the gods
go back
to their regular
offerings,
reality stops
and starts
like the mountain.

*

All the images
            need replacing.
Been such a long time since we did that.
You'd almost think it came this way:
strong borders,
colour filled in right to the edges,
convergence on a point where we stop seeing,
where space
stops, the images that certain.

Okay, but no certainty
            and we plunge into the sea,
no certainty and we never leave dry land.
Try doing *anything*
without the least certainty—certain there are risks, that not
all risks are alike . . . You can't.

*

Be honest,
god of mischief,
god from whose shoulders
the rivers pour out,
farsighted,
freshwater god:
The words
we make and lay
support their
own weight only,

the repetitious clay
of thought
bakes brittle
in the sun.

We're drowning in images.

Surely this is a beginning.
The ground
seems firm enough on which to raise
our young, our paragraphs.
Water's nearby, carving the earth with its name.

Nothing in His Hand

K Hank Jost

Judges 14:5-6

The beer is warm, setting bready about his teeth, gumming up his cheeks. Too many cigarettes, and the sun's just settling down. The feeling is colorless, leaden, tarnished, and uninteresting, so Mark says, with regards to being honest about how he's been, that things are just fine, that work is good and he's managing all the other shit okay.

Evan's come in hot. Crashing to earth at the table, his own beer sloshing over the sides, and immediately he's burning cherry to cherry—pack left open between them, knowing that Mark's always trying to quit—reclining, taking up all the space he could, a braggart's spread, bull and bluster. And Mark eating it soft on the chin—

"Come on. Things are *just* fine?" Evan says.

Mark reaches for another smoke. "Well, I went to pick up the rest of my stuff..."

"Heard about that."

"What do you mean?"

"We're all friends, brother—"

"Did she tell you?"

"I mean, she said it wasn't great..." and Evan believes every bit of it:

Mark's breaking peal—according to her: "But, why do I have to do this?"

And Bella'd said it was because they'd broken up and he didn't live there anymore and she can't believe that even just literally yesterday she can't fucking believe he still left shit behind, his shit's still in this fucking house and he doesn't live here anymore and he still leaves his shit behind because he knows that he'll have to come back for it again and ask her again about why he has to come get his shit and can't they just—but, Evan'd had enough to laugh at, and got plenty of laugh in to feel horrible about it and said then, last night, said, "Can we not?"

"Not what?" And she's upright in the bed, sheets flung off, clavicle blooming a splotchy red he's seeing for the first time, but is pretty sure he's heard Mark talk about how she's got bad skin. And she said, "I can't tell you about my day?"

"Yeah, I mean, yeah, but not if it's about my boy, you know?"

"Oh, it's been plenty of time! I'm surprised you haven't told him yet!"

There's no way. If Mark's gonna find it out, it's gonna be his own doing—and they'll work through it like men, together and against—and leave it solved on the goddamn ground.

"What's she saying? What'd she fucking tell you?" Mark near to getting ready to set to almost really stand up and get a shouting scene going.

But Evan's up first, as always, ducking a bit under the umbrella—but up and asking, "You want another round real quick? We got time?"

"Yeah, yeah, but... wait, what did she tell you? That bitch, what'd she—"

"What're you having?"

"I don't know, whatever's cheapest... I'm gonna call her, fucking bitch."

"Don't do that." Empty pints in hand.

She's got him blocked, anyhow.

Inside, the bartender asks: "What's next?"

"Another IPA and whatever's cheapest."

The bartender returns with a pint and a can.

***

"I'm fucking dying over here, E."

"Yeah?" His voice, rhombohedral through the line, pitiless and terse, "How so?"

"I'm fucking..." Mark trails away from himself—all he's got is guts and they're going, absconding like cowards jumping ship for the easy shock of sub-zero sea. Mark is little but grunt, purge, and mud-brained ache.

Evan's naked in the light. Babywise on the floor, the sun pounding perfect through the curtainless, eastward window of Bella's bedroom. Mark's a dying bovine in his ear. The phone is slick against his cheek: "You still there, brother? What's up?"

It pours, infernal sputter and splash. The stink. None of it's any good, and his hands can barely hold the phone: They're shaking, for one— but they hurt, a chalky throb he's never yet felt. They're purple through the palm and onto the backs, an inner, vascular stigmata drowning what must be, has to be, can be none other than (if indeed he'd hit the fucker hard and over enough to kill the son of a bitch) shattered bone.

"Mark, are you with me? You alive?"

It's an honest question. Evan's surprised that he's alive himself. If it weren't for this sun—ambivalent and prayerless—he'd not have woken enough to answer the phone, much less groan into it.

"Yeah, fuck..." But a silence then. A heaving wait. Evan's not going to pry, so Mark must speak: "I think I really fucked up last night, man... I'm losing my shit..."

"Sounds like it."

"No, like, oh God—" This spurt is shorter, and for that fact all the more violent. "I mean like, dude, I, fuck, I think I fucking maybe hurt somebody really bad..."

The poor bastard was found early, before dawn, not long after what must've happened took place. No ID, but about as bad off as one could be. Dead. The articles all say something-something gang initiation; but Hell, Mark tries hard enough he can close his eyes and see it happening. It was a mess they found. The guy's face wasn't hardly there anymore, teeth all busted out, left on the ground to choke on his own bleeding.

Evan lets Mark get it all out before saying that it's ridiculous, telling him "There's no way, dude. If you got half as fucked up as I did, there's no way," because after that second round in the bar's backyard the night isn't even a blur, it simply isn't at all. Last Evan remembers is coming back with the drinks and Mark staring at his phone, the little glass rectangle alive in his palm, redialing and everything going nowhere.

Bella told him, washing the mason jars of their caked-on overnight oats, at the sink in a t-shirt and naught else but house shoes, fresh and awake and judgy, that he'd been a real wreck. "I don't know. I've never seen you like that. It was weird…"

"What'd I do? What do you mean?" His head aching behind one eye and sweat springing rancid from the rest of him.

"You just like got real handsy, which is fine. I thought you were just going to fall asleep with your head between my legs again. But then you started crying and hollering and then you locked yourself in the bathroom and started calling him over and over and over and—"

Mark got what he hoped was the only round of sick out of him and returned the calls. Made it almost to voicemail before Evan answered: "You alright, man?"

"Yeah, I'm fine, why, what's up?" All short and accusatory, like Mark's bothering him.

"I, uh," roil returning, "I, you called me a bunch, left a bunch of messages last night. You alright?"

"Yeah, I just, did you listen to any of them?"

"No…" Head to his knees, "I'm fucking dying over here, E." But now he's telling him, "No, dude, listen, I really think I—" and the litany, kicking himself in the heart, of the injuries he's woken with this morning: the bruised and busted hands, the shredded knuckles, loose teeth, and smashed lip. There's a cut that's pretty deep on his forehead, and certain places are dull and absent with pain, places that could only hurt on account of something fighting back…

But all Evan's heard now is that Mark's thus far heard nothing. And he's trying not to laugh. Mark's giving over to him about how he thinks he fucking killed a guy, and Evan's doubled-over, swallowing his giggles, thinking how absurd he'd made himself only moments ago: fallen to his knees before her.

"Oh Christ, Evan. Get up! It's not that big a deal."

But he's *no-no-no*-ing. And she, bless her, lets herself laugh at it. He wants to put on a show, she'll play the perfect audience, losing her breath as his pudge shakes with the sobs, blood-starved nub of dick and tight, figgy scrotum retreating—an absolute emasculation, true and earnest and she's laughing.

So, Evan interrupts now: "Mark, you dumb shit, you didn't fucking kill anybody on the train last night. That's fucking ridiculous. We could barely stay upright. Sober you don't have it in you to kiss a bug, much less squash one—you didn't fucking hurt anybody, and you sure as shit aren't capable of killing anyone. This shit happens all the time. Bums die. They beg and then they die…"

"But no, listen." She got it together and descended, hand on his slimy back, "Listen, it was still kinda sweet, okay? I mean weird, but sweet. You were so excited to see me, but you just—like the time you fell asleep with your head between my legs and—"

"I've never done that in my—"

"You certainly have, knucklehead. It's okay. You're just a delicate boy, you know? Sensitive but—"

People have done crazier. People much worse off have done things much stronger than pounding the life out of somebody worse off and already near dying. So, no, it's not crazy to think he can remember, if he closes his eyes and really tries, what it felt like. Guts a little settled now and Evan giving him what-for, Mark can see each blow: a jab that sent the guy reeling, a step to close the gap, and then—he must've gotten a few licks in—a hook that took with it a handful of rotted, driftwood teeth; on the ground then and swift, hard, heavy kicks and stomps to bring it all to peace.

So, Mark says, wiping away his tears, he says: "No, no, man. I think I really fucking hurt the guy. I think I really, really fucked up and beat the shit out of him…"

And he knows he did it all fast and easy. He knows he did it with nothing in his hand.

***

To begin with, this past week, he's been on an atonement kick. Morning after the night of the murder he washed himself of filth in cold water. Stood under the shower's pour, fists at his sides, skin sharp and rising and everything inside climbing to the center—coalescing in a reminder that he is whole, his body is his, and though it all hurts, this too will weather into memory, unjust as that may be. Water to scald, and he took it as long as he could. The boil beating against his back, a deserved scour, cooking him numb. Up until midweek blisters about his shoulders will fill and burst thick salt against his undershirt and collar. The shallow wounds will cake and scab. Mark will itch and itch and itch.

Dry and dressed then that morning, he goes to the coffee shop down the block and begs the confused, exhausted little sprig behind the register to let him pay for the next hundred orders that come in. Tells the baggy-eyed anemic to just ballpark it and run his credit card, to just do it please, for Christssake just fucking do it already, he doesn't care how much it is or how hard it'll be to keep up with!

Every itinerant mendicant to cross his path, until this night now, receives from him their alms of twenty dollars—or as near to it as his dwindling cash reserve'll allow.

And the thought, he's said, haunted him for days. A fear that each of the useless, phone-scrolling police officers on the platforms, buzzarding the turnstiles, stands to recognize him for what he's done, ready to haul him off to pay his honest penance. He imagined himself screaming, crushed and cuffed, that he didn't know he had it in him, that he was drunk, that he's a changed man and meant nothing by it.

But, at work, in the office—or now, again at the bar again—Mark plays a bashful pride: "You should see the other guy," grinned through to tell a story different than the one he believes. Self-defense and innocence all to say he'd done what needed doing and only took it as far as it needed to go. Different in the doing described than what he thinks he'd done, but Evan can see that the motion of the soul he's saying is true enough—watching Mark now on the verge of macking some stringy-haired girl too many years his junior, likely a student or worse.

Mark'd come crashing to earth at the bar a half-hour later than he'd said he would, slapping Evan hard on the back to knock his chest empty and fill it again with gasped foam. Grabbed him coughing into a crushing hug, bellowed then: "How you doing, you beautiful son of a bitch!"

"I'm good. Just fine." Breaking away to sit and catch his breath.

"Nah, I can see it in your face. What's wrong?"

"Nothing, man, nothing. You want a drink?" Evan pulled out his wallet.

Mark waved away the open billfold, "I got these, brother. Your money's no good" And slammed his hand on the sticky wood before him, "Ay! Bartender! Let's get a round over here!"

It's been like this for hours—Mark showing out, being loud—until the place started to fill and the meat market opened.

Evan kept mostly quiet, rising every twenty minutes or so to go to the bathroom and check his phone. Bella's not answering his texts anymore. The silence'd been sudden, blotting immediately after he left her apartment that morning a week ago. The few exchanges they'd managed she'd said nothing more than that she's too tired and needed to sleep early, needed to rise early, had tons to get done and no time this week.

Easy enough, given the dark, to see the spark'd gone out for some reason, so Mark kept feeding them liquor. Even with Evan saying no, the glasses kept filling, kept getting drained and Mark then, with the music loud and the crowd younger, shouts: "The fuck is wrong with you?"

"Nothing, dude. Let's go outside. I need a smoke."

"No, fuck that," hand on Evan's shoulder pressing him back to the stool and fresh shot before him, "What's up your ass, man? When's the last time you got laid?"

"Eat shit," pushing him away, "When's the last time you got laid?"

"E, I'm gonna fuck tonight. Done deal. I'm trying to get you on board right now!" Necked the shot, hissed through his teeth, burped and, "Tell me to fuck off if you want me to fuck off. I'm just saying—"

"Fuck off."

And he did, real quick. A pat on the shoulder and he was gone. And then Evan could freely allow his face to be lit by the phone screen, rereading the few texts she'd responded to, scrolling way up to find the near-nudes she'd slyly sent him a week or two before she broke things off with Mark. He set to thumbing out a thick paragraph, a final blast, one more one last try. By then Mark'd busied himself with the attention of enough empty-bellied, too-drunk young women to land himself in solid rapport with at least one, playing the numbers game until he found the stringy-haired student-or-worse.

Evan watched Mark make his little moves until the phone buzzed in his pocket. Quick and fumbling he brought it up, squinted to read it. Something about the "ick," about how him crying had been too weird, about she didn't want him falling asleep between her legs anymore, about how she's too tired and needs to sleep early, needs to rise early, has tons to get done and no time for anything anymore...

Then the bar is all clatter and crash, shriek and holler, and Mark's head hits tabletop, then floor, then boot.

Now, it is dawn again by the clock's telling—all the aches of a night like the last, again, always again and again, filling head and flesh. The fluorescents above in the drop-ceiling aren't helping, but his pain's no worry so long as Mark's still out.

He'd lost a lot of blood. That boot just about tore his ear off and the liquor had everything in him running thin. Lucky for him, he was quickly limp once the stringy-haired girl's boyfriend commenced to laying in.

Doctor says he's got a fracture in his jaw—hairline, but still—and some teeth shattered. The ear's easy enough to stitch, but they had to get his hands in plaster. Said he should've come in last week and had that done, plus there's some weird infection on his back. And Evan said he'd let him know when he woke up if it was okay for him to stay. Doctor said he didn't care either way, the nurse'll let him know when it's time. But, Evan's staying.

Clock says dawn, but there's no windows here. Evan's eyes are tired and dry and he keeps refreshing his phone screen. There's a webpage open in his browser: a backwater-internet exploitation hellhole and holler that he visits incognito whenever he wants to get his blood up. *shittycitymma.com*. A place where the worst post poorly filmed videos of street violence, bum fights, gang shit, and—occasionally—people fucking in alleyways, on the train, against dumpsters, or flat out in broad public daylight.

He's trying to see if anyone caught Mark's shame on camera and saw fit to post it for the world to find. So far, he's only seen the usual. There's always a couple gems, though. Always the worst of the best of it gets filmed at night: there's a long video of a real evenly matched brawl between two big guys who go quiet once the blows get thrown, they both come out gloriously scathed, out of breath, bleeding proud, and they shake hands after a bouncer at a bar nearby comes to break them up; there's a carjacking, where the driver is rent from his seat like a child, thrown to the ground, and the carjacker speeds off, hits a pole, and blasts out the windshield, his body limp over the hood, sliding down and off a heavy, muffled crumple; then there's the haggard bum cornered against the closed subway doors by a group of teenagers in hoodies, they beat him to collapse and pick him back up, he tries a swing or two but only catches hair and elbow, each time he falls the youths pick him back up and send him to the floor again until he's no longer shielding his face or making any sounds, open mouth and rolled white eyes, all a thick burgundy shine, back to the floor again until he's too limp and gone to rise.

***

Bella'd taken the curtains off the big window in her room the day after kicking Mark out. Six weeks, just about, she's been torn from sleep by the sun's breaking each day—even when it's overcast, the muted change in light is enough. She sleeps naked but she's nothing to be ashamed of, nothing special. And her days, for six weeks now, have been pouring out along, in tandem, concerted and choreographed, with the light: a little work at the desk, emailing emails to the next person that needs an email, and a little about the house. Straightening up. Washing her bowls. Her oats each morning are sweetened with the raw, wild honey Mark'd left in the cabinet.

Heaven

Paul Franz

Scrolling through the photos of the wedding to which he had not been invited, having fallen out with the groom, and with that whole group, Norris felt welling within him a pleasure, but also some kind of sadness. The more he scrolled, the more this sadness took shape. It was a sadness not of envy, he told himself, but, he flinched, of recognition. Everything was too perfect—everyone was too perfectly themselves. It was the afterlife, he told himself.

The wedding was, clearly, a community affair, with roles assigned to each, harvesting the fruits of each one's talents.

Leonard was the officiant—of course. The half-abashed happiness with which he sustained the weight that had been settled on his slight frame showed that Mike and Emma, the bride and groom (with their strangely matched secretive dark eyes, as if they were twins) had judged well.

In another photo, Callum was spinning records as DJ—Callum, the frontman for that fucking terrible streetpunk band, which Mike and Sam had cajoled Norris into seeing that one time, then spent the entire evening at the bar ignoring. This had shocked Norris then. And it was almost obscene, he now thought, knowing the justified contempt in which Mike held Callum's musicianship, that he had cast him in this role. Why reach into Callum's heart and pluck out this frailest image of himself, then force it on a stage for all to see?

It was like resurrection from the dead, Norris thought. How could everyone forgive another, or themselves, so much?

It was Rama who had taken the photographs and posted them. He was a good photographer, really. Even those who played no formal role in the ceremony, he caught being themselves.

There was Josie, beaming with her usual self-regard. There was Sam and his new partner—a man, Markus—together in public for the first time. That is, they were standing so far apart from each other in every photo, so ostentatiously indifferent to each other, that it stated their new link more directly than any embrace could have done. Markus wore a stupid smile. Sam, his usual aloofness, his pseudo-hauteur.

There was Mike's little friend Elias, whom Norris had always liked the best of this set. As always, he looked slightly out of place. He was squinting over his glasses—clear plastic frames the color of tears—but clearly with love in his heart: for everyone present, yes, but also for his new girlfriend, Meg, whom Norris now saw in a few pictures—his first glimpse of her.

She was slighter even than the slight Elias. She wore a billowy purple hippie dress, cinched at her wasp waist. She had billowy, wavy, tangled hair: brown, cropped into bangs just starting to grow out... and a face somehow older than the rest of her and everyone else, as if it had poked through the background of this scene, like some monitory intrusion from beyond. Like the moon through a blue sky, or a cigarette-end through paper.

The whole thing was like a little ship, with its little crew, each man or woman to his or her duty. Yes, Norris thought, shrinking away, it was the afterlife. Everyone had died and been released into their essential form, their eternal and essential body, suffused with self.

Every wedding is an entry into the afterlife, of course. As if to say, this was you, this you have been, this you shall be eternally, you have died into yourself.

And there they stood frozen, in the joy and the terribleness of that.

Good Bones

Sydney Hirsch

Ever since I gave birth, I've avoided looking in the mirror. Whenever I accidentally caught my reflection, I'd get so taken aback—by my paunch, my heavy eyebags, my deep nasolabial folds—that it would bother me for the rest of the day. It was enough for me to look down at my huge stomach when I took a shit. I tried to picture how celebrities would talk about themselves postpartum: how proud they were of what their bodies had accomplished, that the ability to give life was sacred, that you were one with Mother Gaia.

Back in October, my husband and I had plans for our first date in months. He was going to take me out to dinner at the little bistro downtown, the one that we saved for special occasions. When we were first looking at buying this house, he took me there and got us a brownie sundae with one of those fancy Luxardo maraschino cherries on top. Every time I drove past that place I thought of that cherry—molasses-sweet, its shiny flesh so dark it was almost black. I asked Paul if we could share it, but he insisted I take it for myself. I popped the whole thing in my mouth, bit into it, let the syrup fill my mouth like blood.

We got married at the courthouse last year with my parents and his mom and grandma in attendance. We had a cheap honeymoon in Oregon, where we stayed at a seventy-dollar-a-night motel called "Whispering Pines," right outside the Willamette National Forest. We both agreed we'd rather spend money on a home than a wedding with chicken parm plates and a chocolate fountain.

He got a good deal on the house, which was a "fixer-upper" with "good bones," the realtor said. All I knew was that it was close to his company's offices, a half-hour from his mom and sister, and was at least a hundred years old. I liked the tiled bathrooms, the old-fashioned stove in the kitchen, and the master bedroom. I felt like such an adult; in my entire life I'd never once been the resident of a *master bedroom.*

The town closest to our house had a walkable main street and an old private school and a museum dedicated to a somewhat obscure, but local mid-century artist. I looked at the young families, some with tattoos like us, holding hands with their little ones, guiding them through the park. I told Paul I was ready to have a kid. Paul was overjoyed and bought us a new duvet cover from the department store as a gift. We would have lengthy, meticulous sex on the duvet at least three times a week.

My parents called all the time from up east, asking me to send them pictures of the house, the neighborhood, the deer in the backyard. They sent me pictures of my brother's daughter (his second), the peppers growing in the neighbor's garden, and the renovations on my old elementary school. My older sister's twins were starting high school. My mother had taken to wearing floral scarves. My dad had a gray beard.

I told them that Paul and I were expecting over FaceTime. My dad immediately started crying, which made me start crying. I stood up to show them my stomach, held up the ultrasound pictures, and pointed back down to my stomach. *That's what's going on in there!*

That night, Paul and I were under our new duvet cover, our eyes both open and staring at the ceiling, listening to the low thrum of the box fan propped up near the bed.

"Can you feel it already?" he asked, turning towards me. There was a breeze coming in through the crack in the bedroom window.

"The baby?"

"Yeah. Can you feel the baby?"

I put my hand on my stomach. My stomach rumbled.

"Yeah, I feel something," I said, squinting.

I let out a huge fart. We both laughed.

***

Paul and I met at a Friendsgiving party years ago. He saw me pour myself cups of sparkling apple cider repeatedly and asked me if I was sober, too. I shrugged, telling him I celebrate with Martinelli's. I liked his knuckle tattoos that said *BUGS LIFE*. We had sex later that night. I was bashfully New England Irish Catholic, and he was a proud East Coast Italian. Paul played hockey as a kid, and would text me old pictures of him in uniform whenever he was visiting his mom. He played bass in a hardcore band who, at one point, had a record deal. We both lived in shitty apartments on different sides of the city.

I was in love with Paul. He showed me his favorite anime shows and I made him a playlist full of my favorite emo music. Sometimes he would get distracted in the middle of explaining something to tell me how beautiful I was. Whenever we were out together and he politely rejected alcohol, I'd give him a look that told him how proud I was, how we could leave whenever he wanted. I didn't want him to think I wasn't considering him with my every move. It didn't matter that he sucked the life out of me, he gave me everything I wanted. I would think back to the version of myself that was a single woman in her early twenties, eating takeout Chinese food on the floor, working as a receptionist, wondering if I would ever make my way out of all the misery. I found myself wondering if I ever really had, or if it had all just mutated, lulled me into a sense of false happiness. At least I wasn't alone anymore.

I was in labor for seven hours, so my family had time to drive over to the hospital from Massachusetts to be there when I gave birth. I was embarrassed they were going to see everything, but relieved they'd be there right away if I needed them.

We named the baby Chris, after his dad, who died of cancer when he was in high school. Paul usually spoke fondly of his dad, but would randomly vent about what a disciplinarian he could be. He was jealous of my seemingly perfect family: my brother who went to MIT for mathematics; my sister who had twins with a guy once-divorced with three adult children; me, with my notebook doodle tattoos and useless communications degree.

When I first had Chris, Paul was great. He was present. He would pop right up out of the bed and take care of the baby when he cried in the middle of the night, assuring me I'd done all the hard work and it was his turn. He would do things like bring me breakfast on a pink, plastic tray: scrambled eggs, buttered toast, hot coffee with a dash of milk and two Splenda packets.

"You look so beautiful, baby," he once said, his eyes especially blue. My hair stuck out on the sides from sleeping in a ponytail and I had a huge pimple on my forehead.

"I love you," I said. He leaned over and kissed me.

"You should brush your teeth," he said, laughing.

"I will," I said, covering my mouth with my hand. "After my coffee."

I'd turn on *The Today Show* and he'd leave for work after smooching Chris on the forehead and calling him something like "little man."

When Paul came home, he'd surprise me with dinner, usually Caesar salad and fried raviolis with marinara sauce for dipping. He would take off all of his dirty clothes and throw them in the hamper and hop in the shower and then tell me about his day from there, about some inside joke he had going with his coworkers. The baby would be content in his crib and Paul and I would make love before he put on clean clothes.

Every wall downstairs was covered in a glossy wood laminate siding. I came across a child's craft from 1981 in a bedroom, one of those traced-hand Thanksgiving turkeys made out of construction paper. Paul had repaired the giant hole in the kitchen's drop ceiling, but I'd grown to like the '70s-era wallpaper in the bathroom that looked like marijuana leaves. While Paul was working, I was trying to clean, run errands, buy groceries, and keep Chris happy. I would sit in the kitchen and listen to the coffee machine belch out more coffee and forget to refill my mug. I would take naps throughout the day–I'd just stare at the bed from across the room and the feeling would take over and next thing I knew, I'd fallen asleep.

After a while, when the baby cried while we were asleep, Paul would groan and tell me it was my turn. He was the one who had to wake up in the morning, anyway. I knew he was right. I'd prop myself awake and trudge over to Chris and use my breasts to feed him or change his diaper or hold him until he fell back asleep.

After one long day of cleaning up baby shit and vomit, I'd been saving my appetite for an unhealthy salad and fried ravioli, but when Paul arrived, he shrugged and told me he'd forgotten, but that it was also "adding up." He started coming home from work pissed off, already in a bad mood, blaming one of his "retard" coworkers or his boss, and just stare at the TV. I'd offer to make him dinner, and I'd put together something I thought he'd like, and he'd immediately ask why I fucked it up.

I still didn't really know anyone in town. There were the rich people who lived in big stone houses, the eccentric old people who worked at the local businesses, the drug addicts who hung out near the gas station, the younger couples who painted their children's bedrooms a rainbow of different beiges. Paul's sister, Dena, was like that: her kids were named Slate and Bryleigh. I couldn't find anyone else to talk to, so I became best friends with Chris. When Paul fell asleep, we'd sneak off into the master bedroom and take naps, or play, or eat dry Cheerios from a little plastic bowl. Sometimes I'd lie in bed with Chris and work while he slept next to me or gnawed on a toy.

My siblings still lived close to my parents, my sister and her husband right across the street from the Trader Joe's we used to shop at. In my hometown, it still got foggy in the summertime, and they were knocking down the convenience store on the corner and replacing it with a different convenience store. My hometown was boring. All we had was an apple festival every year to celebrate the beginning of autumn.

I would take Chris out for walks in the woods near my house, carrying him in his blue kangaroo-style papoose, kicking away any used hypodermic needles with my sneakers. When we went downtown, I'd buy his favorite treat, something called "Baby Mum-Mum Rice Rusks," for six fucking dollars at the food co-op. I just wanted an excuse to go inside and inhale that health food store smell. I wasn't sure if it was the natural cleaning products they all used, or the scent of the packaging made from post-consumer recycled paper, or the covered bins full of nuts and spices you could buy in bulk.

My mom would ask what I was up to in Pennsylvania, and I'd have to lie and say things like "Trying out pottery classes at the local arts center!" or "I started buying heirloom carrots at the farmer's market downtown, and now I can't go back" just so she wouldn't feel too bad for me. She loved worrying about me, and I hated to give that to her.

The night of the date, I tried "feeling myself." I told Chris about how I'd be wearing a pretty dress to go out to the bistro with his father, and he giggled in his Fisher-Price baby bouncer seat. I scrolled through some of the makeup looks I'd recently saved on Pinterest and worked up the courage to replicate them in my light-up magnifying face mirror. I unleashed my hair from its usual messy bun and shook it free. I tried stuffing myself into a bodycon American Apparel dress I'd saved from college. I could hear the fabric start to give out before I could finish getting it on. Chris fell asleep and I peeled myself out of the dress and put my t-shirt and maternity jeans back on.

I was getting a call from Paul, although he still had a little less than an hour left of his work day. When I touched my phone to accept it, I felt an unpleasant zing of electricity running from the screen to my hand, like ants crawling up my arm.

"Paul?" I asked, hoping it was him on the other line and not one of his coworkers calling to tell me he'd died in a freak accident on site.

"Erin," he said on the other line, his voice low. My heart rate quickened.

"What's going on?"

"I'm at work," he mumbled. "I got in trouble at work."

"What the hell is going on?" I could feel my forehead sweat melting off my foundation.

"Just come here," he said. "I will explain—"

"No," I said. "Tell me right now."

He cleared his throat.

"I fucked up at work today. I fucked up a forklift."

***

I called Bryleigh and told her I needed her a little bit earlier. She told me her mom said it was okay if I dropped the baby off. I asked Bryleigh if she could just come over. I could hear Dena ask her what was going on. I told them, you know what, nevermind about the whole thing. Dena grabbed the phone and insisted I bring the baby over.

"Just let us keep him, just for tonight," said Dena. "Bryleigh can watch him here."

I dropped Chris off with them and drove to Paul's office. It was in a nondescript building outfitted with buzzing fluorescent strip lights. Paul's boss introduced himself to me without smiling. He was short and aging with a huge bald spot, and handsome, chiseled features.

"You look nice," he said, like he was a little bit surprised.

"Thanks," I said, wiping my smeared eye makeup.

"He's wasted," he said.

I opened my mouth to respond, but didn't.

"Drunk. Crashed one of our forklifts into another forklift."

"Where is he?"

"Break room."

Paul's boss took me towards the break room, where we could both hear someone yelling. One of his superiors, or coworkers, I guess.

"You could have *killed* someone, Spada."

Paul immediately looked at me in the doorway.

"Is this your wife?" asked the man who'd been yelling.

I nodded. Paul looked at me, silent.

"This is it. This is the final straw."

I widened my eyes at Paul, and looked back up at the coworker.

"Oh, yeah, it's been a problem for months now," he said, and then turned back to Paul. "She doesn't know any of this, does she, Spada?"

"Months?" I asked, humiliated.

"Months, a year almost," said his boss. "We found it in his truck, remember?"

"Canadian Club whiskey," said his coworker. "Who does that?"

"Oh, fuck you guys, talking about me like I'm not right here," said Paul.

"Listen, I'm sorry," said the boss, coming towards me. "You shouldn't have to see this."

"Don't fucking touch her," said Paul. His boss backed away. The lights sounded like a swarm of cicadas. I wanted to faint. I sat on one of their office chairs made of cheap green tweed and searched for my breath.

"Let's just go home," I said. "Let me just take him home."

"Okay," said the coworker, throwing his hands up. "You take him home. We can have someone drop off his tools."

"I'm not leaving without my tools," said Paul.

"I'll grab his tools," said the boss.

"Don't fucking touch my tools, you piece of shit," Paul was spitting like a rabid dog.

"She can't take him home," said the coworker. "He's dangerous. Call an ambulance."

"I'm not fucking dangerous," said Paul. The coworker was holding him back.

"Stop it, Paul," I said, defeated. "Just shut the fuck up, already."

I turned to the boss.

"Don't call an ambulance," I said. "They're expensive."

"He needs help, lady," said the coworker. "He's not okay."

"We can't just call an ambulance," said the boss, through gritted teeth.

Paul pleaded with me.

"Please, Erin, just take me home," he said. "I just wanna go home. I wanna see my son. I wanna see Chris."

His desperation turned to anger.

"I wanna see my son."

Paul wrestled free from the coworker and proceeded to punch him in the face.

"You just fucked yourself over real bad," said the coworker, squeezing his bloody nose. He turned to me. "And in front of your wife?"

That pissed Paul off.

Before he could pounce on him, the coworker socked Paul in the jaw, filling his mouth with blood. I started crying, genuinely distraught but also trying to distract them. It didn't work.

"We have to get him out of here," said the coworker. "Call 9-1-1."

"If you call 9-1-1, you get the ambulance, the cops, you gotta make a report, all that shit," said the boss. "It's gonna to get the whole fucking company shut down."

***

The boss stayed at the hospital after wrestling Paul into his truck and getting him admitted. He felt bad for me, I guess, since all I had in my life was an alcoholic husband and an eight-month-old baby. We were in some nearly-empty, half-lit seating area. He'd thrown on a worn old sweatshirt and I noticed had one of those "manly" titanium wedding bands on his ring finger. I looked at him and wondered if he had a daughter in high school, one who got good grades and never kissed a boy.

"You guys are young," he said to me, clutching a cup of coffee and sucking from the folded gap in its plastic lid. "You have time. You have plenty of time."

He looked off into the beeping distance of the hospital hallway to avoid making eye contact.

"Yeah," I said. He bought me one of those "cappuccinos" squirted out from a vending machine, made of mostly sugar and hot water. They reminded me of the ice skating rink I used to take lessons at as a kid. I took a sip.

"Erin," said Dena from down the hall. I could smell her perfume before she turned the corner. She was carrying Chris in her arms, her long blonde ponytail bouncing with every step. I grabbed my son from her.

"Chris," I exclaimed. And more softly: "Dena."

Paul's boss set his coffee down, stood up, wiped his hands on his pants, and introduced himself to Dena. She started apologizing to him like her dog had just peed on his lawn. He stuffed his hands in his pockets and glanced back over at me. I rocked my baby in my arms. He turned to leave.

"Uh, good luck," he said.

"Thank you."

We nodded at each other and he walked away.

Dena, Chris, and I got Paul to agree to go to rehab. He gave in pretty easily, mostly because if he didn't accept then he'd have to go to jail. "Inpatient," which meant he was going to sleep there, and be around doctors and probably a bunch of other addicts just like him. The thought of life without him made me cry. I cried a lot. I was afraid it would feel like being alone.

The first time Paul went to rehab, it was because of a public intoxication charge back when he was twenty-five and was found passed out in a field. He said there was a lot of talk therapy there, a lot of "bullshit," but "it did help, I guess." He'd been sober for the better part of five years by the time we met. He started working out more to appease whatever compulsive part of his brain missed drinking. At one point, we tried going vegan, but we both missed cheese too much.

I started wondering if I was the reason he'd started drinking again, or if he'd just been drinking the whole time, and then I started wishing he had just started drinking before we ever met and I could have seen all the red flags immediately and avoided him, but then I wouldn't have Chris.

I didn't want to break up with Paul, but I couldn't figure out how to justify staying in the relationship. I couldn't even decide if I liked him anymore, I just knew I didn't want to be single. I didn't want this house to myself. I didn't want to be a single, fat mother with a baby. I was never going to find someone else to love me.

"You know it's not your fault, Erin," said Dena, outside his hospital room. "He didn't really have that much of a dad, you know? It's probably hard for him to be one."

She placed a finely manicured hand on my shoulder.

"The whole past year was a lie," I said, in the monotone voice I get after crying too hard. Chris was in my lap, grabbing at my limp hair. "I thought I was going to be a mom, and we were going to be happy in our house, and everything would be okay."

"You **are** a mom," Dena said, squeezing my shoulder. I sniffed all the snot back up into my nose.

"He was just getting wasted the whole time," I said, my nose completely clogged.

Dena looked into my eyes, and then down at Chris's. She sighed, her angular edges softening into curved lines.

"That's Paul, honey."

***

It was just me and Chris in the car on the car ride home. We both sat there in silence: him, teething and sucking on his pacifier, my knuckles gripping the steering wheel. We passed the bistro, now closed, and as I glanced into the windows I could see the staff mopping up the floors, wiping down tables, counting cash in the register. I thought of the cherry I was supposed to have eaten that night. I sighed, exhausted, too wrung out to cry anymore. When I pulled into the garage, my headlights bounced onto the wall of poorly-organized power tools and haphazardly placed two-by-fours.

I turned off the ignition and sat in the darkness with Chris for a while. I couldn't bring myself to carry my own tired body, let alone his, into the house. He sat with me, patient as a baby can be, until he fell asleep. Before pressing the button on the garage door remote, I squeezed my eyes shut. I could hear the bark of a neighbor's dog in the distance, the whirr of cars on the road, my son's gentle snores in the backseat. Paul wouldn't be home for a long time now. I closed the garage door, grabbed Chris, and walked into the quiet, empty house. I was surprised it felt so warm.

Bringing the Chair to the Party

Sophie Madeline Dess

If you sit on the chair and finger the wicker, you can make it moan a seven-toner. It's my special chair. There's a whole orchestra in that thing, if you wake her up right. Not that I would really know. I'm not good at music. One time my father tried to get me to play the piano. He sat me down with the expectation of greatness. He said, *Benji, let the sheet music slip into that wide open and empty slot in your brain; let's get those synapses snap-fastening down melodic chains; let's get you Franz Lizst-ing into elegant bistros and select birthday parties.*

But it didn't work out.

It's okay though, because now I have the chair. It's a regular looking chair. But if you sit on it, finger the wicker just right, and get the thing to moan you a seven-toner, it's known as good luck.

Oda asked if I could bring the chair to celebrate his confirmation. His mom was having a party in the park. I didn't know what a confirmation was but I said yeah definitely! I'll bring her.

So I arrive with the chair (and also with my uncle, who can't stop crying) and I see the party's pretty slammed. Oda's mom is holding court. She's standing, silent, smoking a cigarette and spreading gel over Oda's frosted tips.

"Benji!" Oda breaks from her and comes to me. He smells like sweet wax. "Thanks for bringing the chair," he says.

"Sure," I say. "Let's make her sing."

"That'd be great. I've been lying to god," Oda tells me. "I need a new path to luck."

"Of course," I say.

We put the chair on the grass.

Oda prays before he sits on it. There is a look in his eye like he's not quite occupied inside himself as he's praying. Like maybe others are occupying him but not quite that either. Anyway, he prays, unoccupied, and then he sits in the chair. It doesn't make a sound. He tilts forward. The chair is still silent. He tilts backward. Now there's a two-toner. A two-toner is okay, but it's not a seven-toner. Oda knows this. He stands up.

"Goddamn it," he says. "It didn't sing. She's not singing."

"It's okay," I say.

Other boys have a go. Dylan and Zendai and Poppin. Mack and Fitzy sit on it together, laps. The most anyone gets is a two-toner.

I should be paying attention but I noticed, from when I first walked in, that Bunny is standing at the edge of the party, right next to Oda's older brother. She's standing there emitting pretty strong indifference. Towards the chair, us boys, me. I look away.

"Yeah. Don't look at her, Benji," Oda says. "She's a two-toner."

I nod. The thing is, Bunny really is a two toner. One tone comes out of her eyes, and it's superiority. And another tone, cruelty, comes out of her trapezoid, which is the place on her body which will become her hips, but her hips haven't *come out* yet, as my uncle might say, on account of the fact that girls' bodies *come out* and show themselves in a series of 3 revelations, whereas boys' bodies just grow.

Anyway she's standing there two-toning me with her meanness, without even looking or talking to me. I don't pay attention.

I talk to the boys.

Mack comes up to me. "Your uncle is crying, Benji," he says.

"O yeah!" I say. But my uncle's been crying for days. My father says he's on one of those long spiritual journeys that will lack both the will and intelligence to make use of its findings.

"Benji, maybe we should go to him and bring him joy," Oda says.

We all knew what joy was. Not from experience (I'd yet to really feel it), but because Oda's mom is a poet, and she told us: "Oh my god, boys. Joy? Joy is giving yourself up before you have to. Joy is opening up before you're even asked. Joy is a thickening up of a secret self inside you, a sweet ache pulsing at the base of your spine. Joy—"

But she did not go on. We'd all started crying, from fear, from excitement. Like my uncle.

"Nah," I say to Oda. "Don't go to him. He's on a journey."

Oda nods. Then he prays, unoccupied. Then he tries the chair again. Another two-toner.

"Maybe she can sing no longer," he says.

I should refute this. Instead I look at Bunny once more. She's standing so hard like it's real poetry with Oda's brother. She's so calm. Her trapezoid is not moving. She's just standing there. She's not talking. She's looking at him with mint green, chewy eyes. Her floodlight hair. Bright like it's lit-from-the-inside hair. She's not even talking. Not even talking. Just listening to him, Oda's brother. She's looking at him. She's looking at him a lot and not talking. She's listening to him so hard. Not talking. I'm not sure. I feel a heat in my eyes. She's so damn calm.

"Benji—" someone starts. But I don't listen.

"*Bunny,*" I yell it loud across the party. "Hey. Relax yourself girl, just settle down!" … She hardly moves. In fact, no one quite moves. But her trapezoid, I sense, tilts toward me. "Bunny!" I go again. "Relax yourself girl, just settle down!"

There is a bit of silence, you might say.

At this moment my uncle comes toward me: "Benji! *Honey check it out, you got me mesmerized,*" he sings to me through his tears. *"With your black hair and your fat-ass thighs.* Oh Benji. That's a great song. Do you remember that song? Jesus christ."

My uncle sits in the chair.

I knew it would happen as it happened.

When my uncle sits it's right into a screeching seven-toner. The sound is obliterating—a sound so loud, so complex, so beyond the reaches of the self. A primal agony heretofore lain dormant in twisted willow and reed. The bruised howl of a banshee forsaken. Everyone at the party immediately begins to cry. And amidst all this pain, and amidst all this renewal, I have the wherewithal to check: Bunny is looking at us. She's looking directly at me, and at my uncle, and at me. The look is so wicked. She is dry-eyed. I love it. Good lord. I can feel my secret self rising inside me, and I know it then as joy.

Liebestod: A Version

Humphrey Astley

(from the finale of Wagner's Tristan und Isolde,
in which the heroine laments the death of her love)

As though a lullaby dozed on his face
This eye could almost open, feints to open

You see it, don't you, friends?

Now see how white he grows against the black
So high and small, so high and small a point

You see it, don't you, friends?

The lullaby now filling up his heart
Now filling up his chest
Now emptying his lips

You hear it, don't you, friends?

This quiet is not silence but a sound
And does this sound not close me in its arms

This quiet is a sound
This putrefaction pulchritude

And might I breathe it in, and might I breathe
This air as though it were a tonic
Filling up my chest

And might I dive beneath, and might I dive
So deep I crash the far side of the world

I crash the stars

So high and small
So high and small a point
A singularity

You see us, don't you, friends?